Complex of Upper Palaeolithic sites near Moravany, Western Slovakia

INSTITUTE OF ARCHAEOLOGY – JAGELLONIAN UNIVERSITY, CRACOW
ARCHAEOLOGICAL INSTITUTE – SLOVAK ACADEMY OF SCIENCES, NITRA

COMPLEX OF UPPER PALAEOLITHIC SITES NEAR MORAVANY, WESTERN SLOVAKIA

VOL. I MORAVANY-ŽAKOVSKA
(Excavations 1991-1992)

BY
JOSEF HROMADA AND JANUSZ K. KOZŁOWSKI
WITH COLLABORATION OF
STEFAN W. ALEXANDROWICZ, LADISLAV BÁNESZ, BARBARA KAZIOR,
HENRYK KUBIAK, MARIA LITYŃSKA-ZAJĄC, MACIEJ PAWLIKOWSKI,
ANNA PAZDUR, KRZYSZTOF SOBCZYK, JOANNA TRĄBSKA

JAGELLONIAN UNIVERSITY PRESS
KRAKÓW 1995

The publication of this volume has been sponsored by
the Polish Scientific Research Committee (grant no 0954/P1/92).

Varia, CCCXLI
Nr ogólny 1909

ISBN: 83-233-0857-8

Skład i druk: Poligrafia Inspektoratu Towarzystwa Salezjańskiego
ul. Konfederacka 6; 30-306 Kraków

CONTENT

LIST OF CONTRIBUTORS

Alexandrowicz Stefan W.: Academy of Mining and Metallurgy, al. Mickiewicza 30, 30-059 Kraków, Poland

Bánesz Ladislav: Archaeological Institute, Slovak Academy of Sciences, ul. Akademicka 2, Nitra, Slovakia

Hromada Josef: Archaeological Institute, Slovak Academy of Sciences ul. Akademicka 2, Nitra, Slovakia.

Kazior Barbara: Institute of Archaeology, Jagellonian University ul. Gołębia 11, 31-007 Kraków, Poland.

Kozłowski Janusz K.: Institute of Archaeology, Jagellonian University ul. Gołębia 11, 31-007 Kraków, Poland.

Kubiak Henryk: Institute of Systematic Zoology, Polish Academy of Sciences, ul. Sławkowska 17, 31-016 Kraków, Poland.

Lityńska-Zając Maria: Institute of Archaeology and Ethnology, Polish Academy of Sciences, ul. Jana 22, 31-016 Kraków, Poland.

Pawlikowski Maciej: Academy of Mining and Metallurgy, al. Mickiewicza 30, 31-059 Kraków, Poland.

Pazdur Anna: Silesian Technical University – Faculty of Physics Radiocarbon Laboratory, ul. Krzywoustego 2, 44-100 Gliwice, Poland.

Sobczyk Krzysztof: Institute of Archaeology, Jagellonian University, ul. Gołębia 11, 31-007 Kraków, Poland.

Trąbska Joanna: Academy of Mining and Metallurgy, al. Mickiewicza 30, 30-059 Kraków, Poland.

A. A BRIEF HISTORY OF EXCAVATIONS OF A LATE PALAEOLITHIC SETTLEMENT AT MORAVANY ON THE VÁH AND PIEŠT'ANY-BANKA

The first information about mammoth bones finds in the region of Moravany on the Váh and Trnava in western Slovakia comes from the 18th century (Skutil 1938, p. 12). At that time mammoth bone was considered to be a profitable commodity and frequently found its way to the hands of pharmacists and local physicians – a situation analogous to that in China and the Far East where mammoth bones were found in loess. In the region of Považie in Slovakia mammoth bone was believed to reduce fever even as late as the 20th century (Barta 1986, p. 17).

Moravany on the Váh were for the first time mentioned in the professional literature by a Vienese scientist Fritz von Hauer (Hauer 1864). In 1864 the owners of the Moravany castle gave Hauer some finds found on their land in a brick-kiln. The finds were stored in the Imperial Geological Museum in Vienna and some years later Hauer himself described them (Hauer 1871). Five years later Hauer's work was considerably revised (Luschan 1876).

The first information about finds from Moravany published in Slovak appeared in 1864 in a periodical "Obzor" of Matica – Slovak National Historical Society. Already at that time the authors of the article suggested that mammoth bones finds could not have alluvial origin but were the evidence of prehistoric life in the Moravany region.

In 1866, at the 2nd Anthropological and Archaeological Congress in Paris Ferenc Florian Romer – founder of archaeological investigations in Austria-Hungary – delivered a lecture on the chipped stone industry and finds from the region of Morávany on the Váh. A hundred years later these finds were dated to the Neolithic (Banner 1960, p. 710). A well-known Moravian archaeologist Josef Skutil attributed the original discovery of Moravany finds to F. F.

Romer only (Skutil 1957, p. 15; 1959, p. 49) but detailed study of publications and Romer's personal correspondence showed that the finds had been brought to his attention in a letter from his younger colleague Epolyi (Banner 1960, p. 70).

Palaeolithic sites at Moravany were "re-discovered" in 1931 when the baths administrator at Piešt'any and later the Museum custodian Vaclav Vlk assembled a bigger collection of flint artefacts (Eisner 1944-48, p. 19). Vlk distributed the finds among well known experts (J. F. Babor, J. Eisner, J. Neustupný, J. Petrbok, J. Skutil and others). His aim was to prove the relation between the thermal springs in Piešt'any and the density of prehistoric settlement in the surrounding region.

In the 1930 intensive investigations were stimulated by numerous discoveries made by local inhabitants in the loess gulley of Hlboký Jarok. At that time J. Eisner worked as the state conservator in Slovakia but he could not prevent German and Austrian explorers from conducting small excavations and surface collections. The primary objective of those German and Austrian scientists was to prove the existence of dense Germanic population in the region, but they could not help collecting, at the same time, palaeolithic artefacts. Similarly, palaeolithic finds were being collected at Dolní Věstonice in southern Moravia during the same period.

In 1934 M. U. Kasparek, a native of Moravia, published the first tools and white-patinated flakes from the surroundings of Moravany (Kasparek, 1934, p. 35). He sent his material for analyses to the German Charles' University in Prague (Micko 1944, p. 2). J. Skutil, a Moravian archaeologist, published some articles in Czech and German for the newly founded Museum Society of Piešt'any attempting to prevent taking the artefacts out of Slovakia (Skutil 1934 a, b). Later on Skutil wrote the first monograph on the Palaeolithic in Slovakia and Trans-Carpathian Ukraina (Skutil 1935, pp. 110-199, 141-142). The palaeolithic materials which Skutil had found were examined under the direction of A. Prietz (Hajnalová and Krippel 1964, p. 309).

In 1932 J. Petrbok began the exploration of loess profiles at Moravany on the Váh and in 1939 work was continued by a geologist K. Nepletal and later the investigations were joined by J. Neustupný. However, their work did not bring important results.

Because the quantity of palaeontological and archaeological finds from the surroundings of Moravany kept growing (Eisner 1926, p. 16; Hynie 1927, p. 606) archaeological excavations were commenced in 1924 (just as at Dolní Věstonice). This news spread immediately among the general public.

In spring 1935 Lothar F. Zotz – former professor of the Wroclaw University and director of the Archaeological Institute of the German Charles' University in Prague after I. Franz – began investigations and surface collection at Moravany on the Váh. This was directly connected with Zotz's interest in the Palaeolithic

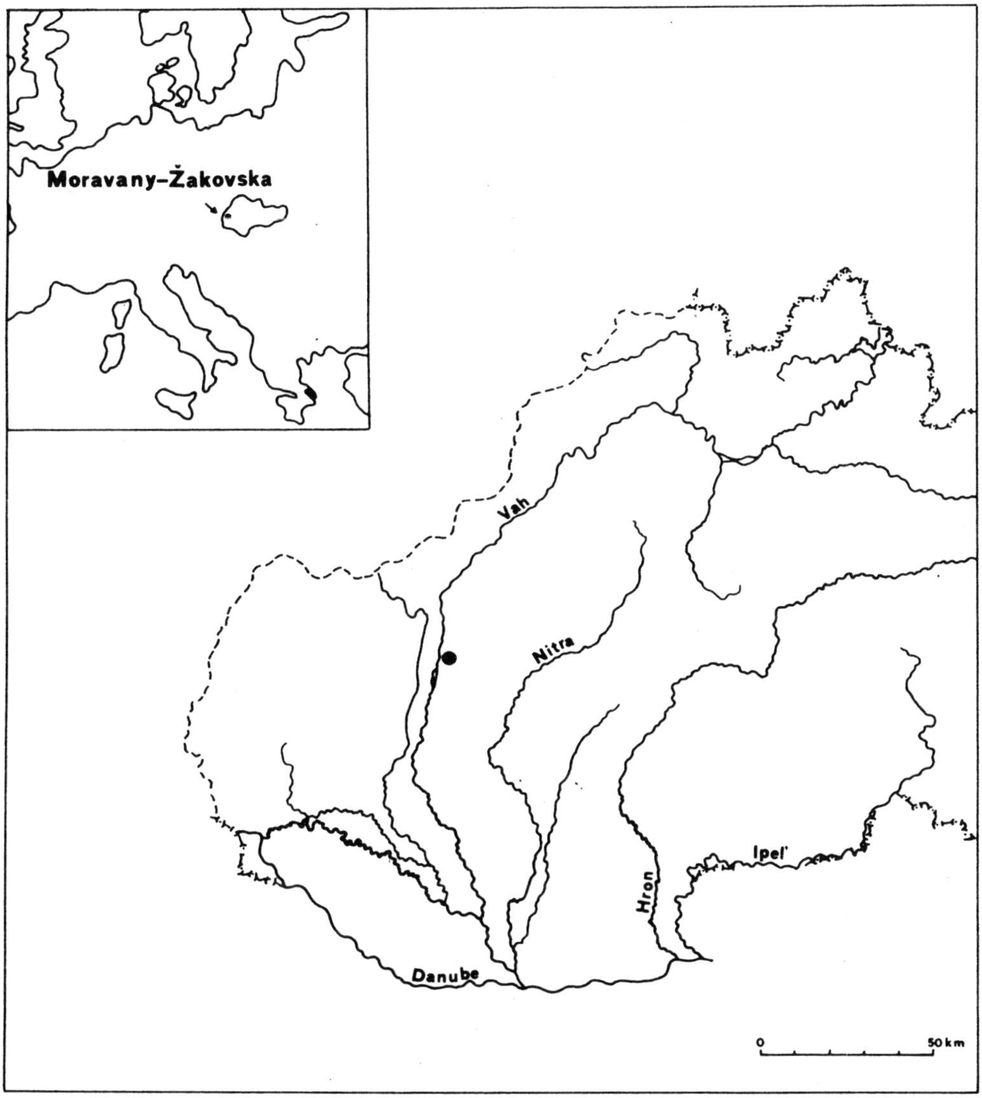

Fig. 1. Index map.

of the Carpathian Basin (Eks 1941; Zotz and Vlk 1939, p. 76; Zotz 1968, p. 5). At the end 1937 Zotz and professor Robert Lais from Freiburg took malacological samples from Moravany (Zotz 1951 p. 185). Around that time investigations of Moravany materials became more intensive. Zotz drew and described in detail almost all the palaeolithic finds from the Museum at Pieštʼany. In December 1937 he conducted minor investigations into the loess profiles at Moravany. In his memoirs Zotz wrote that palaeolithic artefacts at Moravany were "ploughed like potatoes and sold all over the world". Only a small part of that material became the property of the Piešt'any Museum (Zotz 1968, p. 8). Many of these finds can now be seen e. g. in the Magyar Nemzeti Museum at Budapest, in the Naturhistorisches Museum in Vienna, in Mainz, Oxford or in the Metropolitan Museum in New York (Medl 1936, p. 110-111; Foltiny 1973; Novotna 1973).

In 1939 a Czech archaeologist Vaclav Vlk had to leave the Piešt'any Museum. In 1940 L. F. Zotz, appointed by a Berlin Society *Das Ahnenerbe* and with its financial support, continued minor excavations in the region of Moravany on the Váh. With short interruptions these excavations were conducted during the whole period of World War II (Zotz 1941a, p. 204; 1941b, p. 172; 1943, p. 193). Additional support came from Chancellor of the Slovak University in Bratislava. Zotz used the method of small trial trenches which he made in three different areas. Artefacts which had been discovered were then sent to Vienna for analyses. The trial trenches at the sites of Podkovica, Lopata, Žakovska and Dlha brought promising results (Bárta 1960; 1965; 1970; Zotz and Vlk 1939; Zotz 1941 a, b). In 1941 the excavations were interrupted and taken up again in 1943. Artefacts found in these investigations were sent to Prague. The material consisted mainly of the inventory from a Szeletian workshop producing leaf-shaped points. Moreover, Zotz excavated the caves in the same area namely: the Čertova Pec Cave near Radošina (Bárta 1972) and the Velká Jaskyňa in the locality of Dolný Sokol which yielded only Neolithic finds.

The results of Zotz's work in Moravany can be briefly summarized as follows: the discovery of two Upper Palaeolithic dwelling structures on the two sites (Moravany-Žakovska, Moravany-Lopata) whose interpretation however has not been confirmed by further excavations; the discovery of one of the biggest leaf-points workshops (Moravany-Dlha) and finally assembling numerous collections of bones and stone artefacts including two female statuettes which probably come from Moravany-Podkovica and Moravany-Lopata sites (Zotz 1968, Bárta 1984).

The archaeological materials which Zotz had left in Prague after the war were then sent to The National Archaeological Institute at Martin in 1948. One of the female figurines was returned to Slovakia in 1967 but the second has been missing until now. Together with the materials deposited in the Balnaeological Museum at Piešt'any these finds are only a small portion of the original collection.

The first post-war excavations in Moravany on the Váh were undertaken in 1946 by a Moravian archaeologist Karel Absolon (Absolon 1947; Faltys 1946) when trenches were made at other sites.

In the summer of 1949 František Prošek and Vojen Ložek, experts from the National Archaeological and Geological Institute in Prague, started work at Moravany. Their task was to review the material and information thus far and elaborate further long-term conception of investigations in the region of Moravany. A number of trial trenches were made and some profiles were analysed. The results were published in several broader studies (Ambrož *et al.* 1952; Prošek and Ložek 1954; 1955; Prošek 1950; Ložek 1949; 1960). In 1960 survey investigations were carried out at the site of Dlha which aimed at determining the stratigraphic position of the Szeletian leaf-shaped points (Bárta 1970, p. 38). However, the results were inconclusive.

In 1991 the Archaeological Institute of the Slovak Academy of Sciences in Nitra and from 1992 in cooperation with the Institute of Archaeology of the Jagellonian University in Kraków launched an extensive project of investigations into the Late Palaeolithic complex of sites at Moravany on the Váh, Piešt'any-Banka and the surrounding area. Out of approximately 50 sites the site of Žakovska was selected where excavations concentrated in 1991 (Hromada, Barta 1992) and in 1992 (Hromada *et al.* 1993). Subsequently excavations were undertaken on the site of Lopata II where they are being continued. In the future trial trenches and excavations will be made at other sites.

B. GEOGRAPHICAL SETTING OF MORAVANY ON THE VÁH AND PIEŠŤANY-BANKA SITES.

The geography of the region around Moravany on the Váh and Piešt'any-Banka has been presented in the works of F. Prošek and V. Ložek (Ambrož *et al.* 1952). However, new archaeological investigations require the verification of the earlier results of geological and palaeogeographical studies.

The complex of Palaeolithic sites in the region of Moravany is situated on the left bank of the river Váh, at the foot of the Považský Inovec hills. Here the Váh flows through the northernmost part of the Transdanubian Lowland in its eastern margin approximately 8-9 km wide. Originally the Váh was a meandering river with a broad inundation plain. In the investigated region its bed is relatively shallow and the river flows through gravel alluvia branching out into numerous arms, forming islands – sometimes fairly large (e. g. the Kúpelný Ostrov at Piešt'any). In the past the Váh changed its course frequently owing to floods but today the changes of the riverbed are small, restricted by modern flood-control and river-training.

The flood-plain of the Váh in the region around Piešt'any rises from 150 to 170 m. In its western part the Transdanubian Plain is bordered by the Trnava Plateau (220-250 m) gradually rising to form the foothills of the Malé Karpaty Mountains (600-750 m). The Malé Karpaty Mountains separate the Piešt'any region from the Zahorska Lowland. The eastern border of the Váh river basin are the Považský Inovec hills. They are wedge-shaped and oriented along the north-south axis. The southern part of the Považský Inovec reaches the height of about 700 m (Peak Marhat – 749 m), but most peaks do not reach more than 500 m. In spite of this low elevation the relative difference from the floor of the valleys is fairly large – about 200 to 300 m. For this reason we can say that the studied region has a mountainous character as part of a broader landscape. In the southern direction the mountains are become smaller (450 m) and more rounded. In the east the Považský Inovec is bordered by the Nitranska Plateau (200-250 m) and further east by the Nitra river valley. Just like the Váh valley the Nitra valley too is a branching out of the Transdanubian Plain (about 160 m). The mountains of the Považský Inovec rise freely from the wide plain, only in the north they are connected with the Stražovska hornatina mountain range by a narrow pass (360 m) and the Beckovska Gate.

Just as other mountain ranges in the western Carpathians the Považský Inovec has the granite and crystalline core which is the base for the mesozoic mantle. The Považský Inovec mountain range is built of Permian quartzites and quartz-sandstones to the east and south of Moravany on the Váh. Near Moravany there is a narrow strip of gneiss and mica schist and a broader band of granites, a relatively thick complex of limestones and dolomites. Karst occurs around the locality of Radošina with the well-known Čertova pec Cave. These formations belong to the lower sub-Tatran cover.

The morphology of the north part of the Považský Inovec is important. Here, between the Váh valley and the Považský Inovec ridge a plateau, 2 km wide, slopes gently. The plateau rises from 200 m (the edge of the Váh valley) up to 300 m at the foot of the Inovec Mountains. This plateau may have been – according to some early opinions – the uneven bottom of the Paratetidian Sea. Recent excavations do not confirm this old theory put forward by S. Ferenci (1917). The plateau in question is predominantly mantled by mesozoic rocks representing the lower sub-Tatran cover. In the immediate vicinity of Moravany there are Keuper strata mainly laminated clayey slates purple-red in colour, less frequently pink, grey-brown, green or cream coloured.

These beds give way to layers of quartzites and quartz, also sandstone. They are pink or cream in colour. Stratified dolomites appear below these layers. In the southern direction and to the east of Piešt'any-Banka besides Keuper strata there are dolomites and various types of limestones. Friable rocks (especially quartzites and dolomites) show evidence of tectonical processes. The site of Serbalov vrch (also called Rádiový vrch) situated to the south of Banka, is built of probably Miocene conglomerates and sandstones. Further to the south – in the region of Ratnovce – the late Tertiary units developed (probably Pliocene travertines). Small outcrops of Tertiary sandstones have also been registered the area of the Hlboký Jarok.

The whole territory of the plateau is covered by Pleistocene loess layers. The loess layers are sometimes interrupted by island like protrusions of underlying rocks.

The loess cover (especially above the Váh flood-plain) has the thickness of more than 20 m. Now the loess layer covers as well the hilltops on which palaeolithic sites are usually situated. The whole plateau has fairly complex

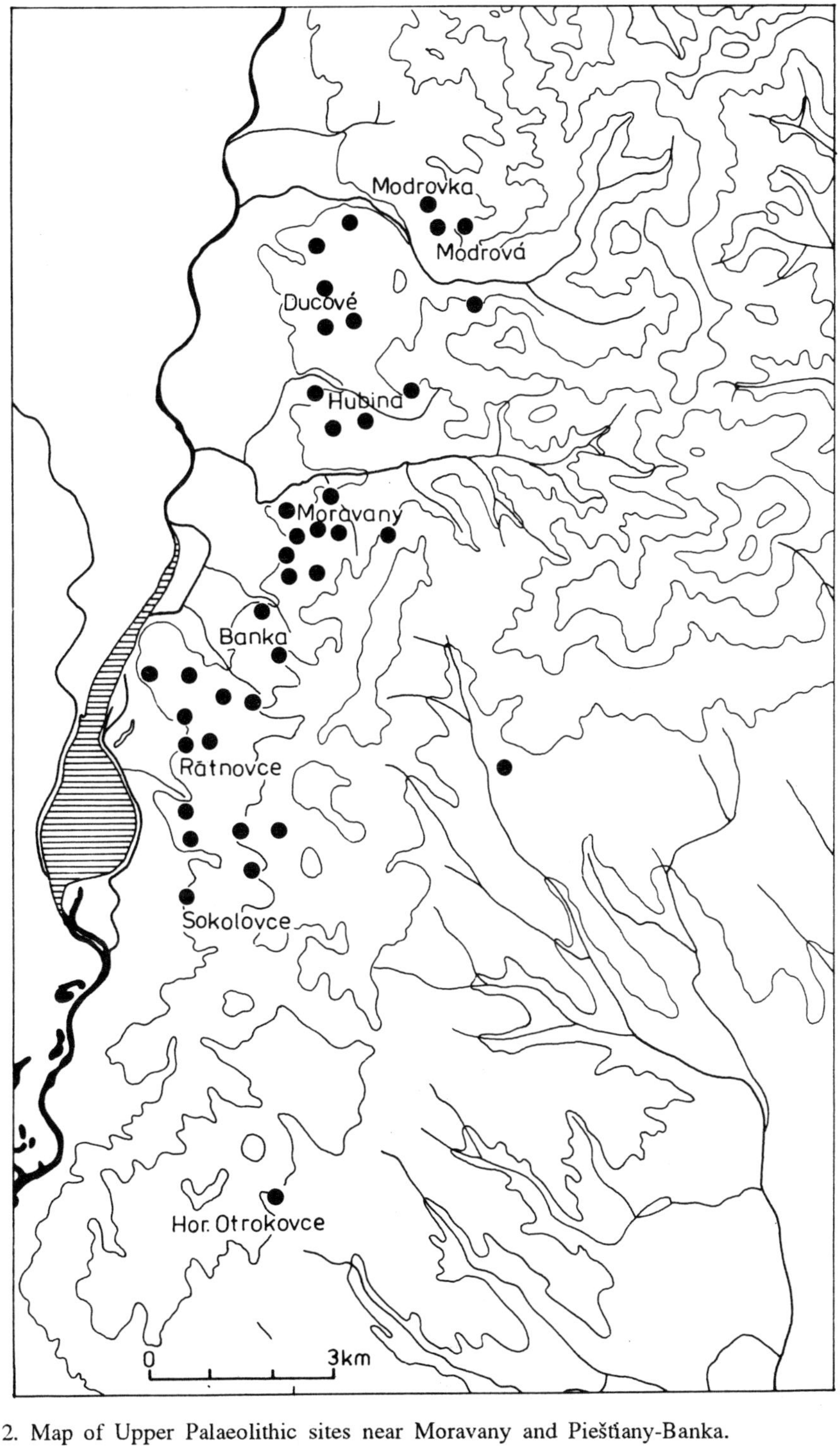

Fig. 2. Map of Upper Palaeolithic sites near Moravany and Pieštany-Banka.

drainage pattern with numerous dry beds of streams descending from the Považský Inovec to the Váh. The character of the underlying rocks as well as the loess mantle enable us to differentiate between older valleys whose shape is rounder and younger V-shaped ravines (sometimes about 20 m. deep). These ravines were formed in recent past over a short period of time. They are the effect of human activity (the Hlboký Jarok is a typical example of a ravine created by old ploughing). These ravines provide now valuable natural profiles showing not only the whole of loess layers but also part of the underlying bedrock (e. g. the Hlboký Jarok). Loess reaches deep into the Inovec hills where it is present not only on flat areas but also in deep valleys where it is mixed up with slope detritus.

In the morphology of this region the boundary of the loess plateau is well-marked, dropping down to the Váh flood-plain. However, this is not the alluvial Váh terrace. The sharp edge of the plateau was formed by the erosion of the Váh.

The wide Váh valley is filled with river gravels whose thickness in the region of Piešt'any, for example, is about 10-12 m. The older alluvial terraces, situated higher up, have not been found. The substratum of the Váh gravels is formed by Miocene sandstones. These gravels are overlain by silts which form the flood-plain of the Váh. It should be added that at many places in the region travertines developed. For example, in the upper part of the Striebornica stream and near some of its tributaries there are remarkable layers of travertine deposits formed near hot springs.

In the region under discussion three natural, well-distinguished units can be identified:

1. the Považský Inovec hills – characterized by specific landscape and almost uniformly covered by forests.
2. the Váh flood-plain – filled with the Váh gravels, almost flat.
3. Loess plateau – separates the two above-mentioned units, and is characterized by a thick loess mantle and a weak relief. It is covered with forest or forest-steppe.

From the point of view of attractiveness for human settlement the best conditions for palaeolithic groups were provided by the loess plateau where numerous Late Palaeolithic sites had been registered. The other two units of the region do not offer such favourable conditions, but they functioned as supplementary areas to settlement.

The loess cover on the western slopes of the Považský Inovec near Moravany on the Váh and Piešt'any-Banka is built of typical loamy loess without layers of coarser sediments. These loesses originate from quartzites, to less extent from shale and limestones violet-brown in colour, also dolomites i.e. from the materials deriving from the sub-Tatran cover. In addition, there is mica which originated from the desintegration of the granites forming the core of this mountain range. The loess cover is not uniform. It sedimented during at least six periods, though it seems that the real number of episodes of loess sedimentation may be even bigger.

Several authors in the past described a large number of terraces at different elevations in the middle Váh basin (Machatschek and Danzer 1924, Vitašek 1934, Andrusov 1932 etc.). But the only morphologically well-developed terrace in the longitudinal section are the gravels whose surface is about 15-20 m. above the Váh flood-plain. In the middle Váh basin outcrops of gravels and sands of this terrace occur frequently. Between Trenčin and Piešt'any the gravel terrace is replaced by the edge of the plateau, morphologically distinct and fairly uniform in elevation. The question of the formation of this plateau – referred to by some authors as pseudo-plateau (Ložek and Tyraček) – is the key issue for students of the development of the Váh valley. All the sediments which build the plateau and were registered in the profiles so far (Moravany on the Váh, Nové Mesto on the Váh, Zamarovce, Ivanovce, Trančianske Bohuslavice) are either loess layers or gravels sedimented by smaller tributaries of the Váh. But these formations have no connection with the fluvial sedimentation of the Váh itself, directly overlying the Pre-Quaternary substratum which had been uncovered by erosion.

C. MORAVANY-ŽAKOVSKA (EXCAVATIONS 1991-1992)

1. INTRODUCTION

This site is situated farthest to north-west in the complex of sites in the region of Moravany. It is located on a mild flattened top of the loess plateau extending along the N-S axis. This is the lowest rise above the pleistocene terrace of the river Váh (about 215 m.a.s.l.).

The first investigations into the site was undertaken by L. F. Zotz in 1941. Zotz made a trench measuring 3x7.5 m. He gave an incorrect name of the locality as "Žarkovska" instead of the correct Žakovska (the name originates from Sunday school pupils who cultivated this terrain as part of agrotechnical training)[1]. Investigations were further continued by F. Prošek in 1949 (Ambrož *et al.* 1952) who made a trench measuring 2×1.5 m.

The excavations discussed in the present work had been undertaken in 1991 by J. Hromada and J. Bárta (Hromada, and Bárta 1992) in connection with the XIIth Congress of UISPP in Bratislava. The investigations were continued in 1992 by a Slovak-Polish team of which the participants are the authors and co-workers who prepared this monograph (Hromada *et al.* 1993).

An area of about 200 sq.m.was explored using a grid of 2×2 m. squares which was the basic unit. Within the squares the finds was three-dimensionally located. Material from wet-sieving, on the other hand, was located with 3-4 cm. thick spits within particular squares. The squares of the grid were arranged in strips a – i (NE-SW axis) and 1-6 and I-VI (NW-SE axis).

In 1991 in the area of the site and in its vicinity geological trenches were made. The obtained profiles were analysed by P. Haesaerts from Institut Royal

---

[1] From the word "žak" – a pupil.

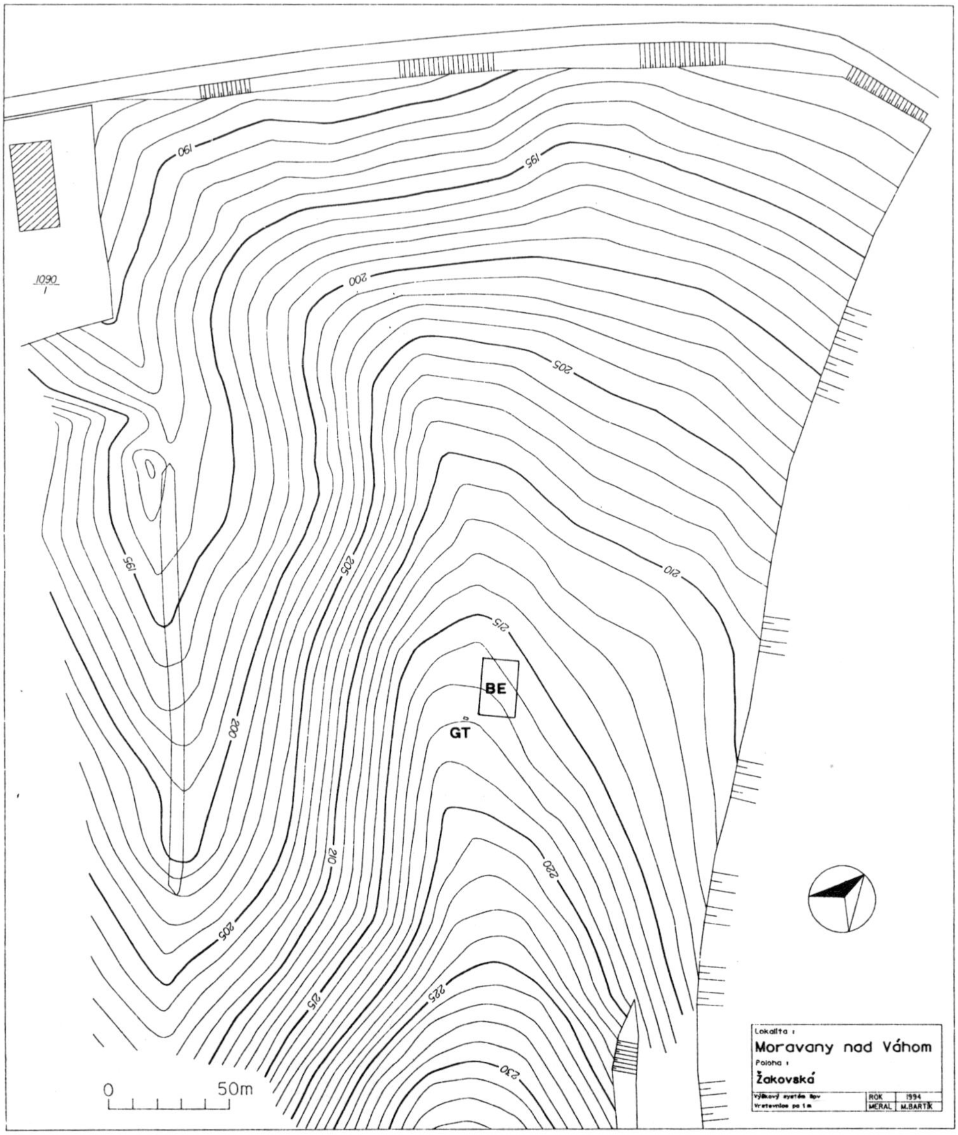

c:\ustation\dgn\mato\moravany\zak2 Oct. 14, 1994 06:12:25

Fig. 3. Moravany-Žakovska. Map view of the locations of excavation blocks 1991-1992 (BE) and geological trench 1994 (GT).

des Sciences Naturelles de Belgique. Regretfully, the results of these analyses have not been described or made available for publication. Because of that in 1994 an additional geological trench (TG) was made. The obtained profile was analysed in terms of stratigraphy and sedimentology by M. Pawlikowski (chapter 2).

2. SITE PROFILE AGAINST THE BACKGROUND OF REGIONAL STRATIGRAPHY

(by Maciej Pawlikowski)

The palaeolithic sites situated on branching out promontories of the upland at Moravany are at present a sub-surface type sites, covered only by thin loess layer. This situation is the effect of intensive Late Glacial and Holocene erosional and denudation processes taking place on the slopes of the upland which borders the valley of the river Váh in the east.

The profiles of practically all palaeolithic sites are strongly reduced and archaeological material occurs almost on the surface. Better preserved sequences of loess and soils separating loess layers are situated on the edges of loess gulleys and ravines cutting the loess upland. The Hlboký Jarok a loess ravine south of the Moravany-Lopata site, was particularly important.

Examination of loess stratigraphy in the Hlboký Jarok were begun already in the course of excavation directed by L. F. Zotz in 1939. The investigations were carried out by R. Leis; however, L. F. Zotz had never used the results nor had he attempted to correlate the profile at the Hlboký Jarok and the profiles of sites explored in the years 1939-1943.

The first attempt at a correlation like this was made by V. Ložek and F. Prošek (Ambrož *et. al.* 1952) when the results of sedimentological and palaemalacological analyses of the profile at the Hlboký Jarok were compared with the profiles of the sites: Moravany-Podkovica, Moravany-Lopata, Moravany-Lopata Zakostolie and Moravany-Žakovska.

The Hlboký Jarok profile was divided into eight stratigraphical series (I – VIII) which were all placed at the Last Glaciation. Loess series from I to IV were ascribed to Würm I loess, series V was identified as tchernozem of Würm 1-2 Interstadial, series VI was regarded as equivalent with Würm 2 (with the transition to Würm 2-3 Interstadial), loess VII, in accordance with this hypothesis, would have corresponded to the wet, tundra episode of Würm 3, and series VIII to the dry and cool episode of this stadial.

The division of Würm 3 loess into two sub-periods: a wetter one (VII) and a drier one (VIII) was justified on the evidence of malacofauna. The yellow-brown loess VII contained loess species (*Succinea oblonga, Columella edentula columella, Vallonia tenuilabris*), steppe species (*Jaminia tridens*), semi-steppe species (e. g. *Pupilla muscorum*) and species of wetter conditions (*Vitrea*). Therefore, malacofauna of loess VII indicates cool, steppe environment with wetter elements and nearby forest habitat. The light-yellow loess VIII contained first of all loess species (*Succinea oblonga, Columella edentula columella*) in the presence of *Pupilla* sp. and *Arianta arbustorum*. This indicates much drier conditions of sedimentation in the period when this loess layer developed.

The profile at the site of Moravany-Žakovska uncovered by F. Prošek was about 2 m thick. Table III from the work by V. Ambrož *et al.* 1952 allows us to evaluate the correlation between the Hlboký Jarok and Moravany-Žakovska profiles:

Depth	Moravany-Žakovska	Hlboký Jarok	Loess series
0–20 cm	arable soil	arable soil	–
20–25 cm	loess sample 4	loess sample 15	VIII top
52–75 cm	culture layer	–	VIII
75–80 cm	loess sample 3	loess sample 14	VIII floor
80–100 cm	loess sample 2	loess sample 13	VII top
100–200 cm	loess sample 1	loess sample 12	VII floor

The table shows that the culture layer from Moravany-Žakovska should correspond to the middle part of loess from the dry sub-stage episode of Würm 3. F. Prošek maintained that the culture layer uncovered at Moravany-Žakovska had a thickness of 23 cm differing from the surrounding loess only by its light-greyish colour. Charcoals, supposedly, occurred only in the eastern part of the trench from 1949. They were associated with a structure which will be discussed later in this work. In our trench the maximum vertical scatter of artefacts approximated the thickness of "the culture layer" from F. Prošek's excavation. We did not, however, recorded the greyish colour of an artefact zone.

In order to verify the stratigraphy of the site described by the authors of investigations in 1949 (Ambrož *et al.* 1952) a geological trench has been made next to the block excavation from the years 1991-1992. The geological trench was about 2 m deep and revealed the following sequence of layers (from the top downwards):

1. arable soil, about 40 cm in thickness,
2. a zone of banded loess with intercalations of homogeneous loess light-brown in colour (20 cm thick),
3. yellow-buff loess, stratified, possibly corresponding to series VIII from the investigations in 1949 (70 cm thick),
4. dark-brown loess, homogeneous, almost unstratified, more silty (its thickness uncovered up to 100 cm). It probably corresponds to series VII from the investigations in 1949.

These loess layers are lying uncomformably on brown fossile soil separated from it by an erosional surface formed by land-slide (5).

In order to make a comparison with the results of analyses from 1949 (Ambrož *et al.* 1952) a wet-sieve granulometric analyses were made for fraction no 2. After drying in the temperature of 105 ^{0}C the samples were soaked in

Fig. 4. Moravany-Žakovska. View of the site and of the Váh valley from Moravany-Podkovica.

Fig. 5. Moravany-Žakovska. View of the site from south.

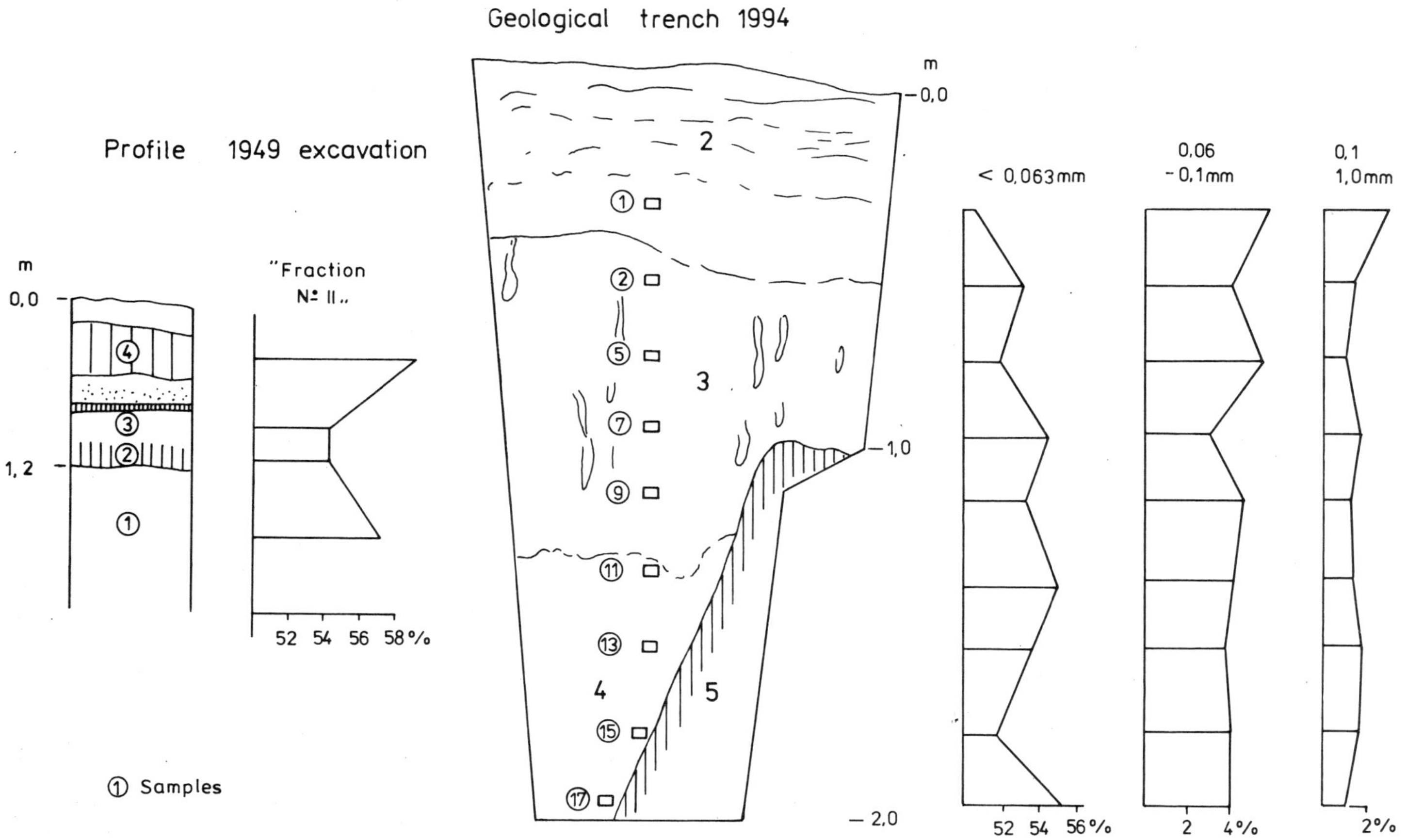

Fig. 6. Moravany-Žakovska. Profiles of 1949 and 1994 exacavations with results of grain size analysis of loess sediments.

Table 1

Results of Grain Size analysis from Moravany-Žakovska (geological trench) (Cf. Fig. 6)

Sample	Grain Size:									
	<0.063		0.125–0.063		0.4–0.125		1.0–04		>1.0	
	weight (g):	%	weight (g):	%	weight (g):	%	weigh (g):	%	weight (g):	%
TG-1 (29.8 g)	26.9	90.27	2.0	6.71	0.4	1.34	0.5	1.68	0.0	0.00
TG-3 (35.0 g)	32.8	93.72	1.6	4.57	0.2	0.57	0.2	0.57	0.2	0.57
TG-5 (32.0 g)	29.4	91.88	2.0	6.25	0.1	0.31	0.1	0.31	0.4	1.25
TG-7 (48.4 g)	45.8	94.68	1.6	3.30	0.4	0.83	0.4	0.83	0.2	0.41
TG-9 (44.2 g)	41.2	93.21	2.2	4.98	0.2	0.45	0.2	0.45	0.4	0.91
TG-11 (53.1 g)	49.7	93.59	2.2	4.70	0.3	0.57	0.3	0.57	0.3	0.57
TG-13 (43.7 g)	40.9	93.59	1.7	3.89	0.4	0.92	0.3	0.68	0.4	0.92
TG-15 (38.0 g)	34.8	91.58	1.6	4.21	0.4	1.05	0.4	1.05	0.8	2.11
TG-17 (33.3 g)	33.3	95.14	1.5	4.28	0.1	0.28	0.1	0.28	0.01	0.02

water for 24 hours. Them fractions were separeted: with the diametre of <0,06 mm, 0.126-0.06 mm, 0.4-0.125 mm, 1.0-0.4 mm and 1.0 mm. After the material had been sorted out it was dried and weighed. Weight in particular fractions was expressed in percentages (Table 1). The obtained results are presented in the diagram in fig. 6. The data obtained indicate that fraction no 2 (Ambrož *et al.* 1952) corresponds to the fraction <0,06 mm in our investigations. In the profile the change in the grain size between samples 4 and 3 can be seen which corresponds to the boundary between layers 2 and 3. Below these the proportion of this fraction increases down to the bottom of the profile.

This confirms the correlation between the data from our investigations and the data obtained in 1949. The correlation between layers 3 and 4 which have been distinguished and loess series VIII and VII from the exploration in 1949 has also been confirmed.

Moreover, at the boundary between layers 3 and 4 the microscopic analysis of the fraction of <0,125 mm has established a decrease in the calcitic concretions content. This is comparable to the observations concerning the boundary between series VII and VIII from the investigations in 1949.

3. SUMMARY OF THE STRATIGRAPHIC SEQUENCE: SEDIMENTOLOGICAL AND MINERALOGICAL ANALYSES

(by Maciej Pawlikowski)

After a layer of about 30-40 cm of arable soil had been removed loess appeared which was then uncovered to a depth of about 1.5 m. Traces of palaeolithic settlement were contained only in the upper part of this loess (at a depth of about 80-90 cm from the ground surface and about 50 cm below the arable layer). Detailed mineralogical and sedimentological analyses were made for this part of the profile in square c3. Here (Fig. 7) banded and unstratified loess alternated. The loess is cut by dessication cracks. At places (the middle part of the profile in fig. 7) a small structure in the form of a broader wedge appeared on top of the banded layer. This may be an icewedge, which is filled with unstratified loess.

In order to perform sedimentological analysis samples were obtained at every 5-10 cm (samples 1-8 in fig. 7) from the part of the profile described above.

The samples were soaked in 1:10 chloric acid solution in order to dissolve carbonates (mainly calcite) contained in the samples. Subsequently, the samples were washed in distilled water in order to drain $CaCl_2$ formed during the reaction. The washed samples were wet-sieved using a 0.1 mm sieve. The material remaining in the sieve was used in analyses. It was dried in the temperature of 40 ^{0}C. Powdered, uncovered preparations were then made. Grain material was placed on slides covered with glycerine. The preparations were

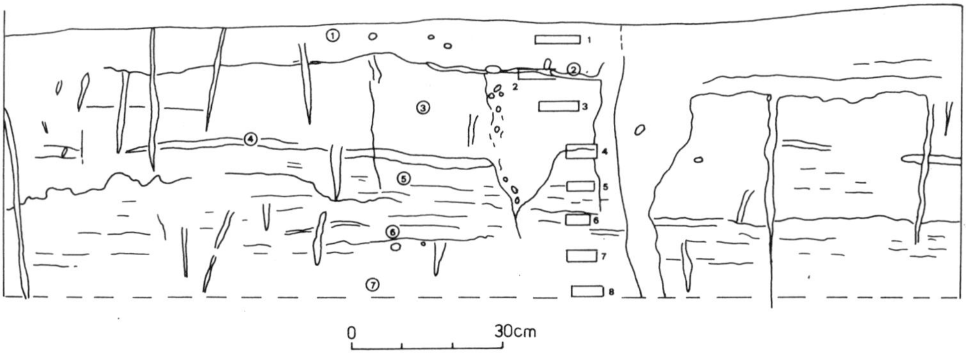

Fig. 7. Moravany-Žakovska. NW profile of square c3 with location of sediment sampling column (1-8). Key to the lithostratigraphic sequence: 1 – fine unstratified loess rich in calcium carbonates, 2 – lenses of clayay loess with calcium carbonate precipitations, 3 – unstratificd yellowish loess, 4 – lenses of brown-reddish clayey loess, 5 – darker slightly laminated loess with amorphous calcium carbonate precipitations, 6 – dark brownish laminated loess, 7 – dark brownish unstratified loess.

analysed using a microscope with side lighting. The grains were counted using the automatic mechanical Eltinor counter. In each sample about 1 000 grains were counted and identified. The results were then expressed in percentages of proportions of particular components. Mineral and anthropogenic components were determined.

The following mineral components were identified: rounded and angular quartz, muscovite, biotite and manganese-ferruginous (Mn-Fe) concretions. These minerals constitute indices of sedimentation, transport and secondary processes which took place after loess sedimentation.

Angular quartz

This quartz is an index of aeolian transport and thus of the original sedimentation of loess. The morphology of quartz grains of this origin is characteristic. Numerous, natural facets are present on the surface of grains resembling intentional scars seen on the surface of stone tools. In this case these are micro-scars, sometimes smaller than 0.01 mm.

Rounded quartz

Quartz of this type, with a characteristic polished surface, is a mineral which indicates water transport. Rounded quartz in the examined material represented two types: rounded, clear, originally angular aeolian quartz, and yellowish, opaque quartzes originating from the washing out of detritic rocks other than loess. The two types of rounded quartz were counted together.

Muscovite and biotite

The genesis of these minerals is complex. As laminated minerals they could have been both transported by wind as well as washed into the investigated sediments. Their analysis showed variability of these components both in the profile and in the archaeological horizon.

Mn-Fe concretions

They can be regarded as an index of moisture of the climate during loess sedimentation and of the oscillations of the water-bearing horizon. They precipitate mainly in sediments at the contact of ground water with the air contained in the sediments.

Results of the quantitative analysis of the above-mentioned mineral components are given in Fig. 8. The proportion of rounded quartz grains is the highest oscillating in the range from 51 to 65% of the volume of a given fraction, increasing towards the top of the profile. Angular quartz grains are less numerous oscillating from 8 to 25% of the volume. Their proportion decreases in the direction of the top of the profile (Table 2). Muscovite accounts for 9% at the bottom of the profile to 1,5% at the top. Biotite occurs only in the lower part

Table 2

List of tested mineral and anthropogenic components
(volumetric %). Profile NW of sq. m. c3 (cf. Fig. 7)

Mineral components

Sample no	1	2	3	4	5
1	65.5	20.3	1.5	–	12.5
2	67.3	17.3	2.8	–	8.6
3	63.4	14.1	6.3	–	15.8
4	60.1	21.2	7.3	–	3.7
5	65.6	8.0	6.1	–	19.0
6	55.5	19.0	9.5	3.1	6.3
7	53.1	25.5	14.8	4.2	2.1
8	51.6	24.1	9.4	1.8	2.8

1 – rounded grains of quartz, 2 – angular grains of quartz, 3 – muscovite, 4 – biotite, 5 – concentrations of Mn–Fe oxides

Anthropogenic components

Sample no	6	7	8	9	10
1	–	–	–	–	–
2	0.9	–	0.9	0.6	–
3	–	–	–	–	–
4	1.8	3.6	0.9	0.8	–
5	–	–	–	–	–
6	1.5	1.5	2.8	–	–
7	–	–	–	–	–
8	–	–	–	–	–

6 – burned grains of quartz, 7 – charcoals, 8 – bones, 9 – microflakes of radiolarites, 10 – traces of haematite

of the profile. The ratio of manganese-ferruginous concretions varies considerably from several up to 22%. Their increased proportion occurs after consecutive maxima of angular quartz ratio, correlating with the levels of a lower frequency of angular quartz grains.

The sedimentological analysis confirms the domination of processes of water transport re-deposition of material on the slopes over aeolian sedimentation. When we look at the proportions of the various mineral components we find that a period of sedimentation with a greater importance of aeolian agents (cf.

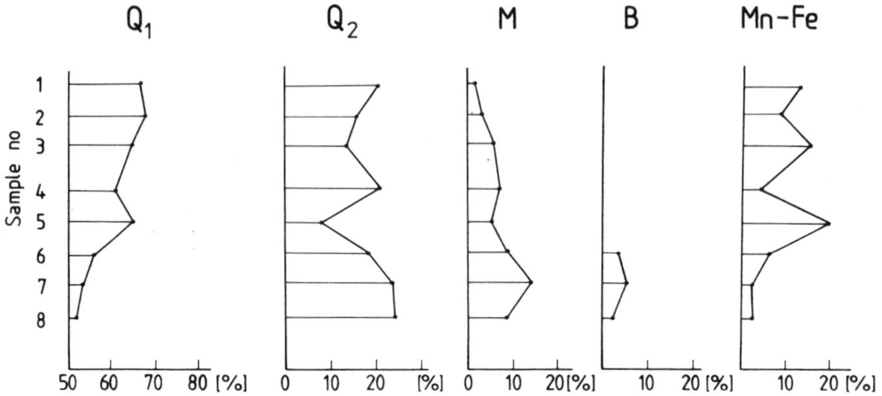

Fig. 8. Moravany-Žakovska. Results of quantitative analysis of mineral components in the fraction 0.1-0.01 mm in the profile of square c3 (see Fig. 7). Key: Q1 – rounded quartz, Q2 – angular quartz, M – muscovite, B – biotite, Mn-Fe – manganese-ferrigineous precipitations.

samples 8,7,4 in Fig. 7) was followed by periods of re-deposition of detritic material in the conditions of intensive slope-wash, probably in warmer, at any rate wetter, periods (samples 6,5,3). In these periods manganese and iron oxides appear indicating the rise of the water-table.

4. MACROSCOPIC AND MICROSCOPIC ANTHROPOGENIC COMPONENTS IN THE SITE PROFILE

The projection of macro-finds onto northern profiles of particular strips (Fig. 9, 10) shows that the initially fairly restricted range of their vertical distribution becomes gradually divided into three levels:

- level I at a depth of 0-5 cm,
- level II at a depth of 8-15 cm,
- level III, with fewer finds, at about 20 cm.

When macrofinds were projected onto western profiles of the site the separate levels were less evident, especially in the east part of the concentration of stone finds. The levels are better demarcated in the western part of the concentration (Fig. 11-12). This distribution of finds suggests that in the eastern part of the concentration finds occur in a shallow depression in the palaeosurface.

The projection of levels containing finds onto the sedimentological profile shows that concentration of finds frequency corresponds consecutively to the

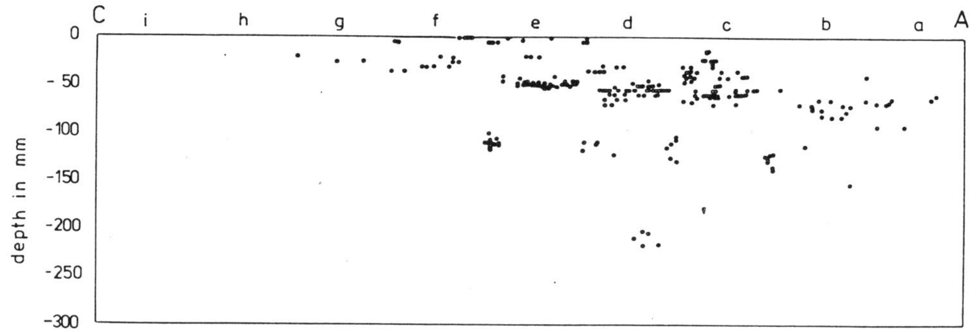

Fig. 9. Moravany-Žakovska. Projection of macro-finds onto northern profile of strip g3-a3 (cf. profile AC on Fig. 15).

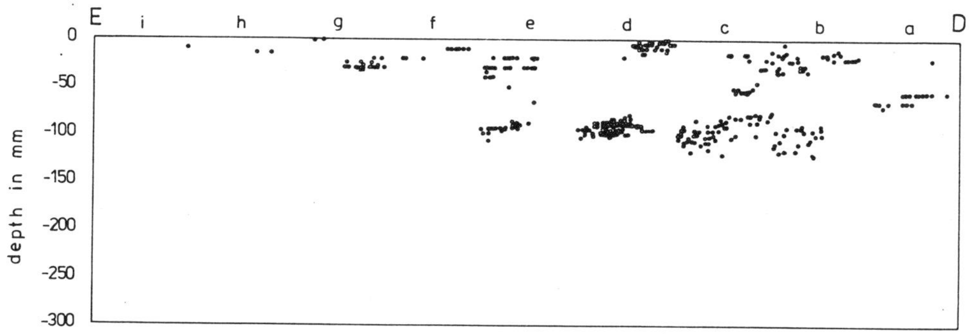

Fig. 10. Moravany-Žakovska. Projection of macro-finds onto northern profile of strip a1 (cf. profile DE on Fig. 15).

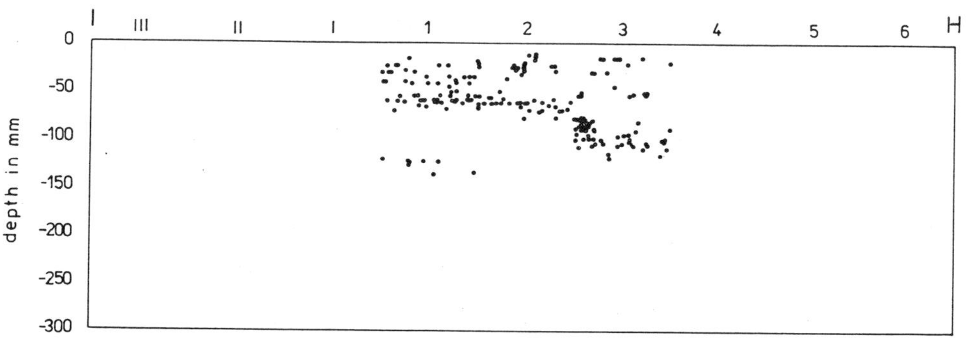

Fig. 11. Moravany-Žakovska. Projection of macro-finds onto western profile of strip c (cf. profile FG on fig. 15).

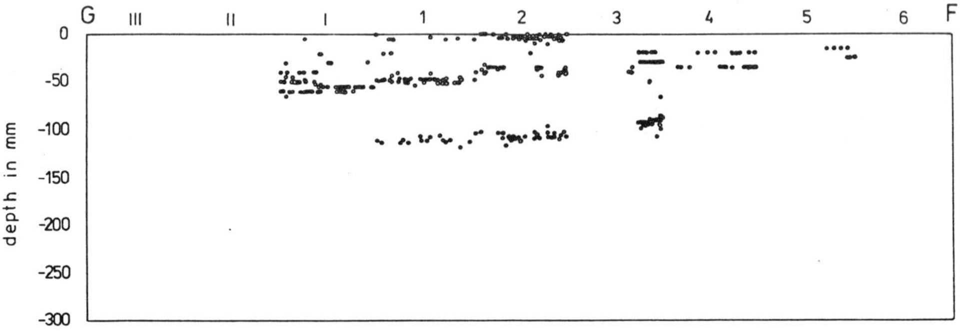

Fig. 12. Moravany-Žakovska. Projection of macro-finds onto western profile of strip e (cf. profile HI on fig. 15).

level with sample 1 (level I), with sample 2 (level II) and the level in between sample 3 and 4 (level III).

The samples obtained from the investigated sedimentological profile were analysed in terms of the content of anthropogenic components in the microfraction isolated after wet-sieving. The following have been established to be anthropogenic components:

Burnt quartz

Quartz burnt in a hearth (max. temp. up to 750°C) has a characteristic matt surface; it is semi-transparent or sometimes even opaque. The surface can be cracked with traces of thermal splitting off. The colour of this quartz varies. The quartz heated in the reducing atmosphere (hearth centre) is grey. When burning took place in the oxidizing atmosphere the quartz can be reddish or buffet (hearth edge). In this group there occurs both angular as well as rounded quartz.

Charcoals

Burnt charcoals are easily identified in the fine fraction thanks to their distinctive tissue structure. Sometimes these tiny pieces were washed out far away from the hearth.

Small chips of lithic raw materials

Chips of lithic raw materials come from the chipping of stone tools. Sometimes they are smaller than 0.1 mm. The raw material can be identified at magnifications of 100-150× (Pawlikowski 1990, 1992). Small chips of red (R) and green (G) radiolarite were identified in the investigated material.

Bone chips

Thanks to their characteristic structure bones are easily identified under the microscope. The analysed material contained both pieces of spongy bones and compact bones. Besides unburnt bones there were also burnt pieces. All the types of bone chips were counted together.

Haematite

Grains of cherry red medium-crystalline haematite were found in the samples from the culture level.

Figure 13 shows the frequency of the anthropogenic indices in particular samples (in percentages of volume of a given fraction) from the site profile.

Anthropogenic indices are present in samples 2, 4 and 6. Lithic microchips are missing in sample 6 and fine chacoals do not occur in sample 2.

When the vertical distribution of anthropogenic indices in the microfraction (0.1 mm) is compared with the levels of macro-finds frequencies an interesting picture is obtained:

1. the uppermost level /I/: the frequency of macro-finds does not correlate with the intensity of anthropogenic indices in the microfraction,

2. level II: the frequency of macro-finds correlates closely with the upper level (sample 2) of occurrence of anthropogenic indices in the micro-fraction,

3. level III containing few macro-finds corresponds to the intensity of anthropogenic indices in sample 4,

4. the lowest level of occurrence of anthropogenic indices in sample 6 has no corresponding macro-finds.

The frequency of anthropogenic indices in respect of quantity is as follows:

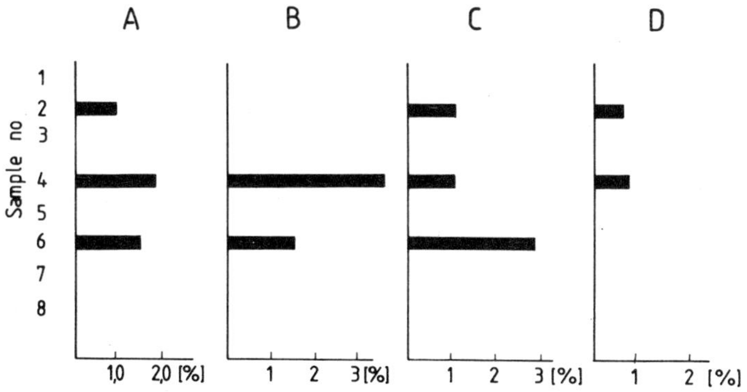

Fig. 13. Moravany-Žakovska. Results of quantitative analysis of anthropogenic components in the 0.1-0.01 mm fraction: profile of square c3 (see Fig. 7). Key: A – burnt grains of quartz B – charcoal flakes, C – micro-fragments of bones, D – radiolarite chips.

Burnt quartz

The distribution of burnt quartzes in the profile is uneven (sample: 6, 4, 2). Their maximum quantity was recorded in horizon III (sample 4) and does not exceed 1.8% of the volume.

Charcoals

They occur in the lowest archaeological horizon and in horizon III. In horizon III they are twice as numerous as in the lowest horizon (Table 2, Fig. 13).

Bone fragments

Their presence was established in horizons II-IV. The biggest quantity (2.8% of the volume) was recored in the lowest horizon.

Radiolarite chips

Radiolarite chips were identified in archaeological horizon III and II and did not exceed 0.8% of the volume. All the chips were of red radiolarite.

Three archaeological horizons (II-IV), each with a different quantity of identified anthropogenic indices, were distinguished in the profile. This suggests varying intensity of settlement and – first of all – various types of activities in particular phases of occupation of the site. Comparison of mineral components and anthropogenic indices indicates that:

1. The lowest archaeological horizon (IV-sample 6) formed during a drier period when the flow of detritic material was weaker but aeolian sedimentation more intensive.

2. Archaeological horizon III (sample 4) formed at the beginning of a drier period preceded by intensive flow of sediments and the rise of the ground water table i.e. by a wetter and probably warmer phase.

3. Archaeological horizon II (sample 2) formed in the conditions similar to those preceding the formation of horizon III i.e. at the border between a drier period and a wetter and probably warmer phase.

Horizon I is not reflected in the microfraction. In all likelihood this has been caused by the location of the area from which the sample was obtained. The activities performed in that area did not belong to the type of activities producing anthropogenic indices such as related to hearths or stone working. It is also possible that because the palaeomorpholgy of horizon I was slightly uneven the sample 1 was located directly below or above the archaeological horizon.

5. SCATTER-PATTERN OF MACRO-FINDS AND HORIZONTAL VARIABILITY OF ANTHROPOGENIC INDICES

Analysis of the distribution of macro-finds (lithic artefacts, stones and bones) shows that the scatter-patterns in levels I and II overlap exactly (Fig. 14). Together they form a sub-circular structure measuring 14×15 m. It is only when artefacts have been projected onto the profile that finds from the two levels could be separated. This, however, could not be done in all the squares since the palaeomorphology of the surface on which artefacts rested is uneven. For this reason the distinguishing of the two levels is in some projection impossible. Because of that finds from level I and level II are described together. It should be added that in respect of technology and morphology the artefacts are strongly homogeneous. Finds from level III are few, forming a small concentration mainly in squares d1 and d3. These are first of all some debitage products.

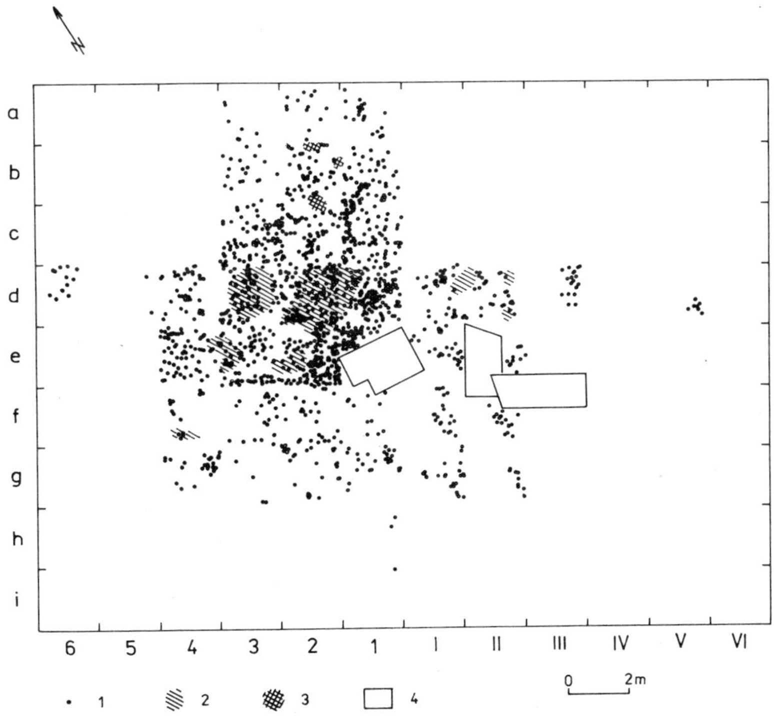

Fig. 14. Moravany-Žakovska. General scatter-pattern of macro-finds. Key: 1 – lithic artefacts, 2 – bone concentrations, 3 – hearth indices in the micro-fraction, 4 – previous excavations.

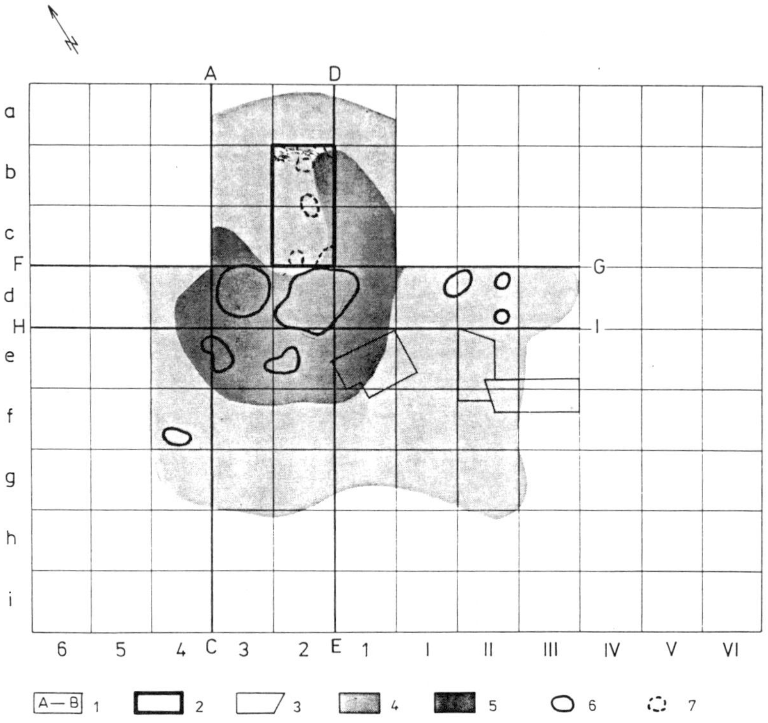

Fig. 15. Moravany-Žakovska. Macro-finds concentrations limits in archaeological horizons I and II. Key: 1 – profiles with projections of macro-finds (Figs 9-12), 2 – area of horizontal sampling for sedimentological and anthropogenic indices analysis, 3 – L.F. Zotz and F. Prošek excavations, 4 – concentration in archaeological horizon I, 5 – concentration in archaeological horizon II, 6 – bone concentrations.

Level I contains a sub-circular concentration of finds measuring 12×14 m (Fig. 15). Besides lithic artefacts in the marginal parts of the concentration there are small clusters of bones in squares f4, dI and dII. Moreover individual unworked stones occur in squares f3 and dII. Fine bones and several unworked stones discovered in the trench made by F. Prošek, in square eII, were also contained in culture level I. The problems of location of finds from the trench made by L. F. Zotz in 1941 have been mentioned earlier in this work.

The scatter-pattern of finds in level II is wholly contained within the frame of the structure in level I. The small thickness of the loess layer separating the two levels corresponds to the short period separating the two settlement events. This indicates that when the site was re-settled its surface still showed some traces which enabled the same location of the camp in level I as in level II.

The structure in level II is crescent-shaped, about 8 m in diametre, opening to the north (Fig. 15). The outline of the cluster of finds in level II suggests that a habitation feature (a light tent), which has not been preserved, must have existed here corresponding to the empty space surrounded by the crescent of macrofinds. This feature, then, could be an example of habitation structures positioned excentrically in relation to the subsistence activity area – in accordance with the classical model by A. Leroi-Gourhan (1967).

The concentration of macro-finds in level II comprises as well bone clusters. Two small clusters are located at the periphery, in in squares e2, e3 and a larger cluster of bones is in squares d1, d2 and d3. The latter concentration overlaps with the centre of the sub-circular khshemenitsa. In the clusters of bones larger, unworked stones and fragments of haematite were present.

When the frequency of major tool groups in level I and level II are compared no essential differences in the horizontal distribution of artefacts are established. Flakes, blades and retouched tools occur in equal proportions in the same squares (Fig. 16). An exception is the presence of, primarily, blades in the bone concentration in square dII where however tools are absent (Fig. 17). In square f4, on the other hand, there are both blades and tools. The maximum blade frequency was recorded in squares d1 and e1 both in level I and level II (Fig. 18).

In both levels the scatter-pattern of artefacts in subsistence activity areas is similar. There is little spatial variability in the types of subsistence activities. A certain difference can be seen in the more central position of the butchering area in level II and its more peripheral position in level I in relation to the whole concentration of finds. Other activities including chipping and reshaping of stone tools, also the preparation of mineral dyes are not attached to any particular areas. There is no distinct zone of dumping rubbish.

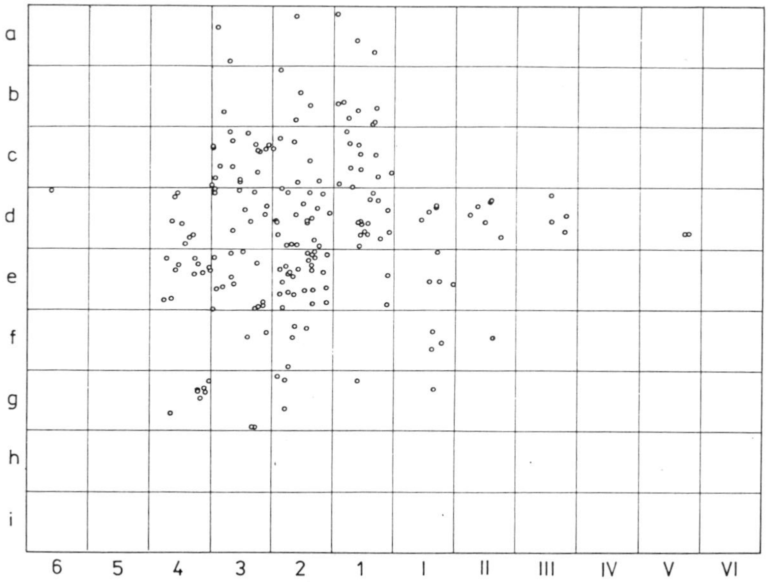

Fig. 16. Moravany-Žakovska. General scatter-pattern of flaces.

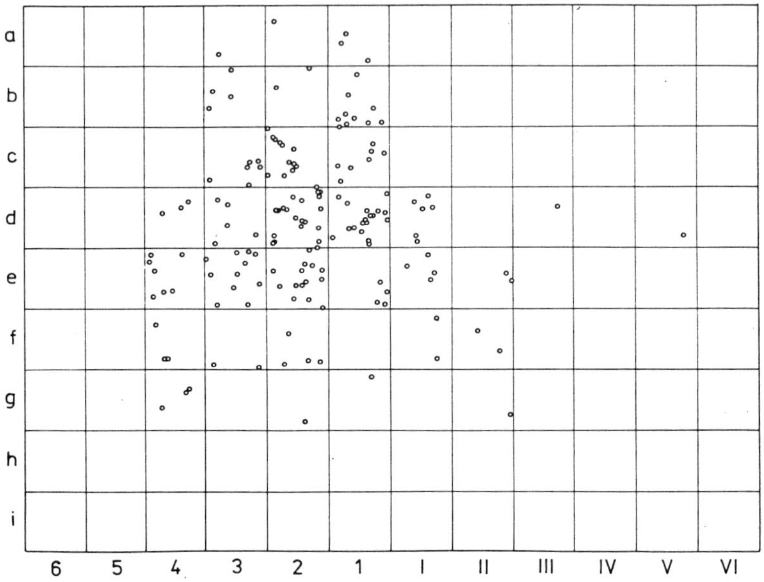

Fig. 17. Moravany-Žakovska. General scatter-pattern of retouched tools.

An area of 8 sq m in squares b2 and c2, corresponding to lower level II, has been examined in detail. The surface is basically without macro-finds. It is located in the concave part of the crescent formed by the concentration of

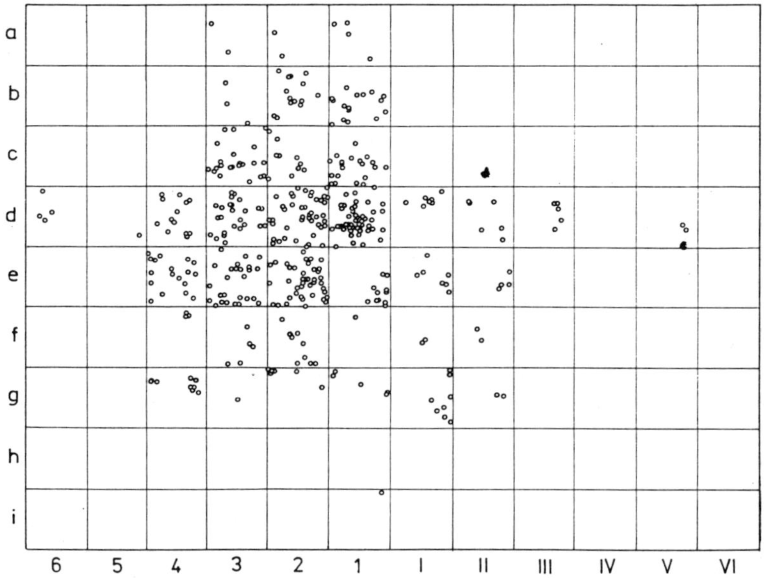

Fig. 18. Moravany-Žakovska. General scatter-pattern of blades.

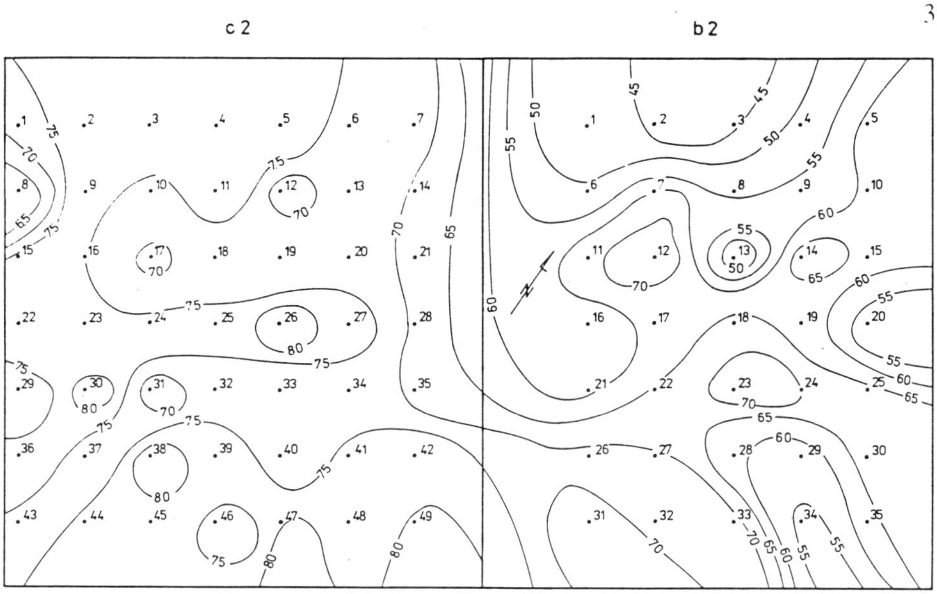

Fig. 19. Moravany-Žakovska. Isolines of frequency of rounded quartz grains in squares b2 and c2 – archaeological horizon II.

macro-finds. This zone could be interpreted as the hypothetical location of the habitation feature in level II (Fig. 15).

Samples were obtained from this zone in order to perform sedimentological analysis of mineral composition and anthropogenic micro-factors using similar methods as for the profile of the site. The samples were obtained at 87 points of intersection of 25 cm grids.

Sedimentological analysis showed that rounded quartz grains are unevenly distributed ranging from 45 to 83%. The isorhythmic map of quartz grains distribution (Fig. 19) shows that loess material was washed into the investigated sector from SE and NW. This suggests that in this part of the site a small basin was present in the palaeomorphology of the site. The position of macro-finds in the longitudinal and transversal profiles of the site confirms the above interpretation. The ratio of sharp-edged quartz is higher in square b2 which is caused by the fact that the horizontal cut is in this place at an angle to the palaeomorphology of the surface in level II. As a result samples in square b2 were obtained slightly above the true surface of archaeological level II. Above this level in the profile an increase in the ratio of angular quartz is recorded (Fig. 20). In addition a higher content of muscovite and manganese-ferruginous concretions is recorded in parts of square b2.

Analysis of anthropogenic indices examined the same elements as in the profile of the site. Conclusions drawn on the basis of this analysis are very

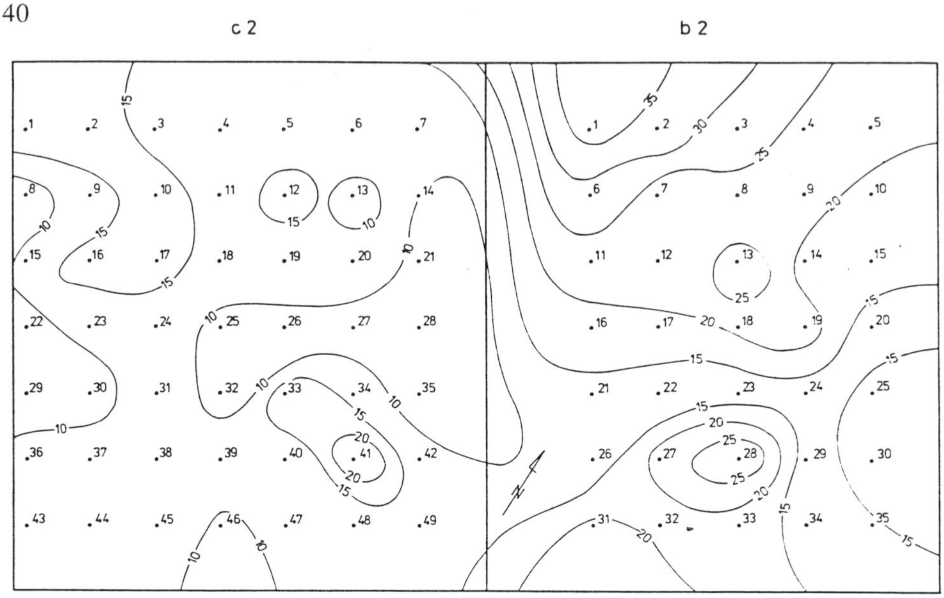

Fig. 20. Moravany-Žakovska. Isolines of frequency of angular quartz grains in squares b2 and c2 – archaeological level II.

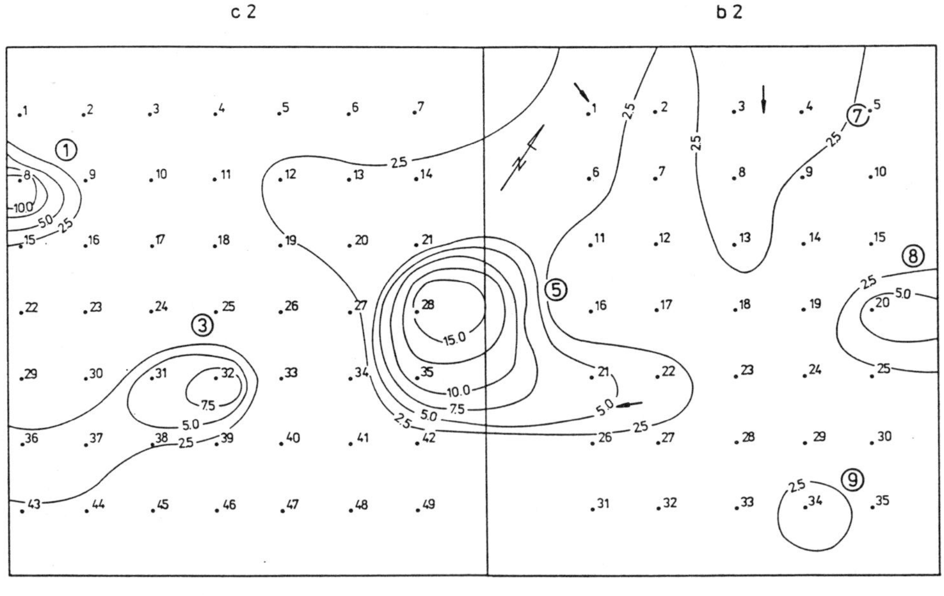

Fig. 21. Moravany-Žakovska. Isolines of frequency of charcoals in 0.1-0.01 mm fraction (squares b2 and c2 – archaeological level II).

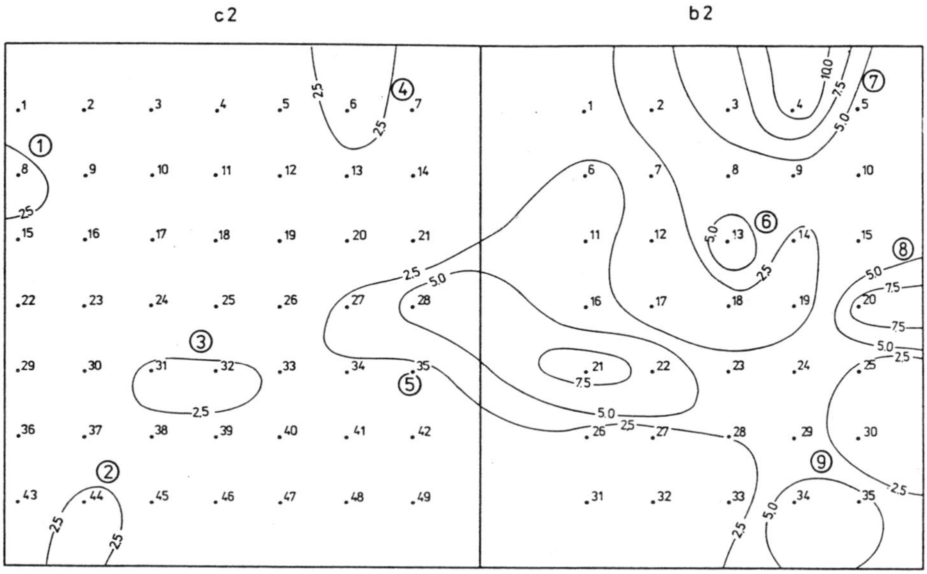

Fig. 22. Moravany-Žakovska. Isolines of frequency of burnt quartz grains in 0.1-0.01 mm fraction (squares b2 and c2 – archaeological level II).

interesting namely: although there are no evident structures indicating the presence of hearths, yet analysis of fire indices in the micro-fraction has enabled us to locate areas of burnt quartz and charcoals on the surface without macro-finds. There are 9 areas like this marked by burnt quartz (Fig. 21) and 6 areas marked by fine charcoals (Fig. 22).

These areas can be interpreted as traces of four hearths, used for a short period of time, situated at the boundary of squares b2 and c2 (they are dennotated in figs 21 and 22 as nos 5, 7, 8, 9). They were most probably situated close to the entrance to the habitation structure; the hearths may not have been large, quickly washed out by rain, or – possibly – these were only charcoals brought from outside which were later washed out. The hearths zones were slightly displaced within an area of about 8 sq m. For this reason quartzes and micro-charcoals are in this case a much more precise index of traces of burning than evident traces of hearths.

The results of analysis of other anthropogenic indices including fine radiolarite chips and pieces of haematite have established that they surround the main hearth structure dennotated as no 5 at the boundary of squares b2 and c2. From this we can infer that near the entrance to the habitation structure there existed a zone where traces of fire, burning of haematite used as a dye and using radiolarite tools concentrate. Next to this zone, in squares b3, c2 and partly c3 there are zones with no anthropogenic traces at all which may have served as "zones de repos".

6. EVIDENT STRUCTURES FROM THE INVESTIGATIONS OF L. F. ZOTZ AND F. PROŠEK – CRITICAL REMARKS

In 1941 L. F. Zotz discovered a rectangular feature sunk into the ground, measuring 1.4×2.5 m, in a 2.5×10 m trench. According to Zotz's description (1942) this was a trough-like basin filled with darker loess, a regular rectangle in outline. The structure contained stone artefacts and bones and tusks of mammoth (Fig. 23). The feature was probably located at the boundary between square e/f III and e/f II in our grid (cf. Fig. 15).

In 1949 F. Prošek made a trench, 1.6×2.0 m, which cut the northern corner of the trench made by L. F. Zotz in 1941; Prošek's trench was probably located in square e II in the present grid. A drawing made by F. Prošek, published by J. Barta (1987), shows that a patch about 0.9 m in diametre was discovered in the southern part of the trench which was cut by the trench dug by L. F. Zotz. (Fig. 24). However, the patch had not been recorded by Zotz or shown in his drawing. The patch contained charcoals and according to Prošek "remains of beams, 7 to 10 cm thick, placed diagonally on one another (Ambrož *et al.* 1952 p. 88). Because artefacts "occurred above the beams" a supposition was offered that "this was a wooden grate-like floor" *(op. cit.).*

The proximity of this structure – unrecorded by Zotz although it was cut by his trench – and the rectangular patch described by Zotz led Prošek to the conclusion that "the hut discovered by Zotz was not an independent structure but a part of a bigger construction to which belonged as well the floor discovered in 1949" (Ambrož *et al.* 1952).

In the course of our exploration no traces of structures like pits, basins or any remains of bigger charcoals, which could be parts of timbers or boards, have been discovered. A supposition can be made that the hut supposedly discovered by L. F. Zotz may have been a washed-out hearth. Moreover, his claim that the feature was a regular rectangle in outline arouses a number of doubts as to authenticity of his observations. Among the many palaeolithic habitation structures (cf. Sklenař 1975, 1976; Desbrosse, Kozłowski 1994) there are no rectangular features sunk into the ground. The allegedly rectangular dug-out from Timonovka in Russia (Velichko *et al.* 1977 p. 111-117) has turned out to have been part of a polygonal ice-wedge structure.

The floor recorded by F. Prošek may have been the remains of a hearth with superimposed furrows from ploughing. We have recorded furrows like this in the arable layer in several places east of our trench. Locally (i.e. above culture levels) artefacts have also been found in the arable layer.

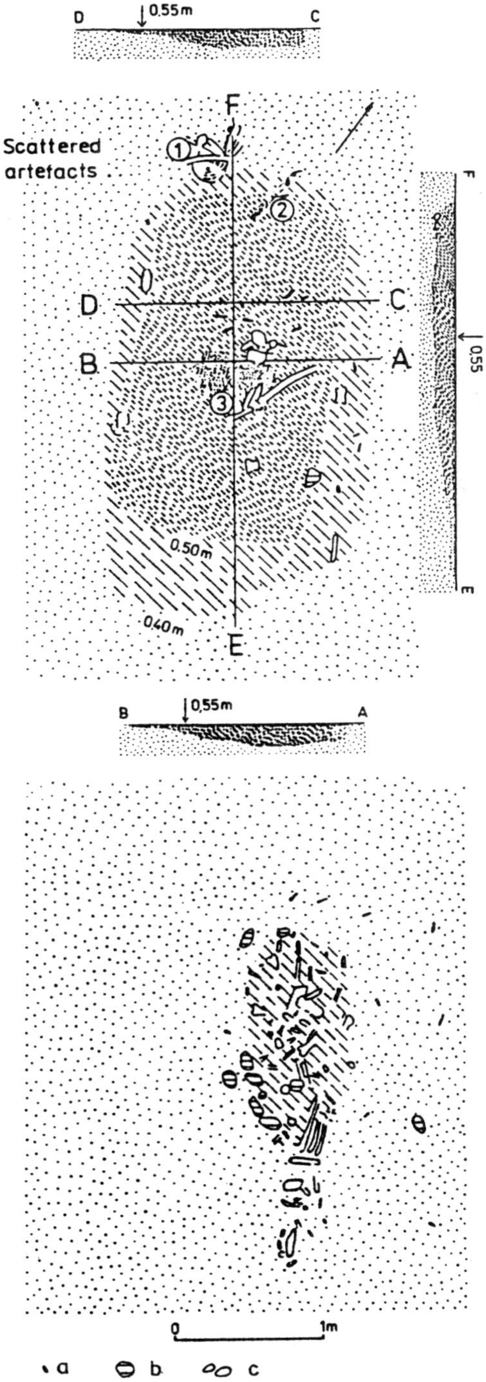

Fig. 23. Moravany-Žakovska. Map of the excavation of L. F. Zotz. Key: 1 – artefacts, 2 – stones, 3 – bones.

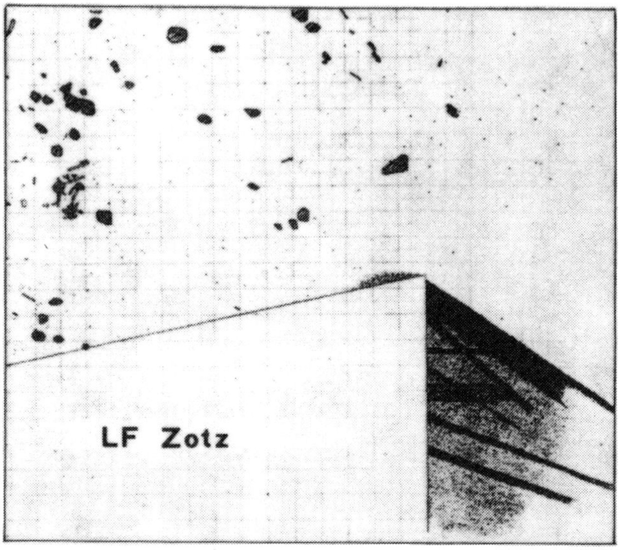

Fig. 24. Moravany-Žakovska. Map of the excavation of F. Prošek (acc. to J. Bárta).

In any case the finds from the trenches dug by Zotz and Prošek should be ascribed to our cultural horizon I. Finds representing horizon II were missing in the area of the two trenches. If we were to interpret the traces uncovered by Zotz and Prošek as, partially, remains of a hearth then such a hearth should have been situated at the SE periphery of the kshemenitsa from cultural horizon I.

7. CHIPPED STONE ARTEFACTS

7.1. General inventory structure

The general inventory structure is given in Table 3. In the total number of 1477 chipped stones the low ratio of flakes (14.8%) in comparison with blades (31.5%) and fine chips (31.3%) is characteristic. These ratios suggest that on the site blades were produced from already decorticated cores and that retouching and rejuvenation, of tools were carried out. The above structure is typical of base camp type sites (often with an even higher ratio of retouched tools) located outside the areas od raw materials deposits (J. K. Kozłowski 1982).

Table 3

Major technological groups

	N	%	% (without unworked pieces)
Cores	19	1.2	1.3
Flakes	242	14.9	16.4
Blades	513	31.5	34.7
Flake fragmentsand small flakes	510	31.3	34.5
Retouched tools	194	11.9	13.1
Chipped lithics – total	1478		100
Unworked pieces	150	9.2	
Total	1628	100	

7.2. Raw materials

The raw materials structure is provided in Table 4. The decided dominance of radiolarites (86.8%), a considerable proportion of specimens of alluvial origin suggest that the main source of raw materials were the gravels of the Váh bed. The survey of these gravels near Piešt'iany (near the bridge at Piešt'iany) confirmed the very high frequency of radiolarites in alluvial beds predominantly red radiolarite which was most often discovered on the site.

Other raw materials occur in small quantities: mainly quartz and quartzite (1.6 and 1.3%), flints and limnoquartzites (1.2 and 0.8.%). The former group of raw materials is also local, of alluvial origin, the latter group are meso- or extralocal imports. Flints belong to mesolocal raw materials originating, most probably, from southern Poland. Limnoquartzites, on the other hand, may come from central and southern Slovakia. Other raw materials which are present in trace quantities are probably local (gneiss, opal, porphyry) just as individual finds of unworked rocks and minerals which were not used in chipping industry (calcites, limestones, sandstones, haematites, mudstones, limonites and pirytes – Table 5). Some of these raw materials were used as mineral dyes. The results of their analysis are discussed in chapter 7.8.

Table 2

Raw material structure in particular technological groups

Raw material	Cores	Flakes	Blades	Flake fragments and small flakes	Retouched tools and burin spalls	Ground stone industry	Total N	%
Radiolarite	18	230	493	480	184	–	1405	94.6
brown	–	2	2	–	–	–		
grey	–	10	20	21	1	–		
yellow	1	8	9	6	–	–		
black	–	1	–	–	–	–		
red	9	128	284	270	108	–		
red/green	3	18	24	13	8	–		
green	5	58	143	116	45	–		
red with veins	–	1	1	–	–	–		
red/grey	–	–	1	1	–	–		
red/yellow	–	–	–	–	4	–		
indeterminate	–	4	9	53	18	–		
Flint	–	2	6	5	6	–	19	1.3
Menilithics hale	–	–	4	8	–	–	12	0.8
Opal	–	–	–	1	–	–	1	0.07
Limnoquartzite	–	2	6	5	1	–	14	0.9
Quartz	–	3	2	4	–	1	10	0.7
Quartzite	1	3	1	4	1	–	10	0.7
Gneiss	–	1	–	–	–	–	1	0.07
Porphyry	–	–	–	1	–	–	1	0.07
Quartz-piroxene-chlorite shale	–	–	–	–	–	1	1	0.07
Sandstone	–	–	–	–	–	6	6	0.4
Indeterminate	–	1	1	2	–	1	5	0.3
Total	19	242	513	510	192	9	1485	

Table 5

Unworked pieces of stones

	N	%
Quartz*	16	10.9
Quartzite*	11	7.5
Radiolarite (red)*	10	6.8
Shale**	5	3.4
Limestone***	8	5.4
Calcite**	2	1.4
Sandstone*	17	11.6
Mudstone**	1	0.7
Porphyry*	1	0.7
Haematite***	64	43.5
Limonite***	7	4.8
Pirite***	5	3.4
Total	147	

* Used in chipped stone industry
** Not used in tool production
*** Used as dye

7.3. Cores

Technological and morphological analysis of cores is given in Tables 6-8. Among 19 cores as many as 18 are made from radiolarite and only one specimen is made from quartzite. Initial cores are few (3), all made on thermal fragments, with little preparation. There is only one pre-core with lateral bifacial preparation. The remaining cores are residual single-platform (6), double-platform (4) or cores with changed orientation (6).

Double-platform and 90° degrees cores represent the most advanced phase of core reduction. Besides the dominant change of orientation (even three times), rejuvenation, among others by detaching a tablet, was ocassionally performed.

Table 6

Single platform cores

Stage	Platform	Striking surface	Right side	Left side	Back	Distal end	Plate
1. Initial	unprepared	narrow (2 scars)	–	–	–	–	14:2
2. Initial	prepared	2 scars	–	–	–	edge	14:3
3. Initial (pre-core)	formed by single blow	bifacially prepared	crest	crest	–	crest	14:1
4. Advanced	formed by single blow	broad	–	prepared	prepared	punctiform	15:1
5. Residual	formed by single blow	broad	prepared	–	edge-shaped	–	15:2
6. Residual	formed by single blow	subconical convex	extended striking surface	–	–	punctiform	15:3
7. Residual	broken	narrow	prepared	prepared	crest	crest	15:4
8. Residual	prepared	conical	extended striking surface	extended striking surface	extended striking surface	punctiform	19:1
9. Residual	formed by detaching of a tablet	conical	extended striking surface	extended striking surface	extended striking surface	punctiform	16:3
10. Residual	prepared	subconical striking surface	extended striking surface	extended	–	punctiform	19:2

Table 7

Double platform cores

Stage	Platform I	Platform II	Striking face I	Striking face II	Right side	Left side	Back	Plate
1. Common striking surface	prepared	prepared	broad	–	extended striking surface	extended striking surface	cortical	16:4
2. Common striking surface	formed by single blow	prepa-red	flat, broad	–	cortical	cortical	cortical	17:1
3. Separate striking surfaces	formed by single blow	edge-shaped	flat, broad	flat, broad	extended striking surface	extended striking surface	2nd striking surface	16:2
4. Separate striking surfaces	prepared	edge-shaped	flat	flat	prepared	prepared	2nd striking surface	16:1

Table 8

90° Cores

Platform I	Platform II	Striking surface I	Other striking surfaces	Right side	Left side	Back	Plate
1. prepared	unprepared (perpendicular to the first platform)	flat	surfaces flat (90°)	–	2nd platform	unprepared	18:1
2. prepared	unprepared (on the back)	flat	flat (90°)	2nd platform	prepared	unprepared	18:2
3. formed by single blow	formed by single blow (on the left side)	flat, triangular	flat, triangular	extended striking surface	2nd platform	2nd striking surface (90)°	18:3
4. formed by single blow	unprepared on the back	flat, (crossed by scars from changed orientation)	convex	cortical	2nd striking surface	2nd striking surface	18:4
5. formed by single blow	edge-shaped	3rd platform	triangular striking face with common directions of scars	2nd platform	extended striking surface	2nd striking surface	19:3

7.4. Flakes and blades

The total number of flakes (242 specimens i.e. 14.8% of the whole assemblage) with very few cortical specimens (15.8% of all flakes) indicates that decorticated nodules or pebbles were supplied to the site. Among 64 flakes with cortex only 10 specimens are wholly cortical (Table 9). Flakes with lateral cortex (20 specimens) and flakes with distal and proximal cortex (21 specimens) occur in more or less equal proportions.

A decided majority are flakes without cortex (179 specimens) with predominantly parallel scars on the dorsal side (15 specimens). Specimens with perpendicular scars come next (Table 10). On this basis we can say that the flakes come from the processing of blade-flake cores or, possibly, from the change of orientation of these cores.

Table 9

Cortical flakes

	N	%
Wholly cortical	10	15.9
3/4 cortical	9	14.3
1/2 cortical: lateral	20	31.7
distal	10	15.9
proximal	1	1.6
1/4 cortical	10	15.9
With peripheral cortex	3	4.7
Total	63	

Table 10

Dorsal pattern of flakes

	N	%
Uni-directional	115	49.6
Opposed direction scars	15	6.5
Perpendicular scars	56	24.1
Centripetal scars	21	9.0
Tablets	16	6.9
Crested flakes	9	3.9
Total	232	

Flakes show considerable variability in respect of platform types, platform edge and percussion points. The hard hammer technique seems to have been employed but, at the same time, the location of percussion points was random. Platforms formed by a single blow and facetted platforms are equal in number (Table 11). Linear and punctiform platforms come next followed by unprepared platforms. Nearly half of the platforms have a well-marked percussion point and nearly half show traces of careful preparation of the platform edge prior to flake removal (Table 11).

Further confirmation of the use of the hard hammer is a decided ascendancy of specimens with a well distinguished bulb (more than one third) and specimens with a visible although less distinct bulb. Flakes with *esquillements* on the bulb and with a well marked lip are less numerous. The latter specimens may possibly suggest that exceptionally a punch was used.

The flakes are small in size. The maximum length does not exceed 6.4 cm with the mean length of 2.41 cm. The width does not exceed 6.1 cm with the mean width of 2.22 cm. The mean thickness is 0.55 cm. In shape the flakes

Table 11

Flakes and blades: butt types

Butt type	Flakes		Blades	
	N	%	N	%
1. Cortical	11	5.1	4	1.6
2. Unprepared	22	10.2	30	12.1
3. Single-blow	66	30.7	106	42.9
4. Faceted	61	28.4	41	16.6
5. Dihedral	9	4.2	10	4.1
6. Punctiform-linear	43	20.0	53	21.5
7. Indeterminate	3	1.4	3	1.2
Total	215		247	
(missing proximal part)	(27)		(266)	

Table 12

Flakes and blades: percussion features

Butt type	Flakes		Blades	
	N	%	N	%
A. Percussion point				
invisible	115	54.5	169	65.5
well marked	96	45.5	89	34.5
Total	211		258	
B. Butt edge				
unprepared	114	51.8	102	37.9
prepared	106	48.2	167	62.1
Total	220		269	
C. Type of bulb				
well marked	87	44.8	99	41.1
weakly marked	50	25.8	76	31.5
esquillements	26	13.4	15	6.2
lip	26	13.4	46	19.1
removed	5	2.6	5	2.1
Total	220		269	
D. Platform angle				
0	40	19.3	60	24.9
<45	6	2.9	5	2.1
50-80	3	1.4	1	0.4
80-90	76	36.7	68	28.2
90-100	43	20.8	37	15.3
100-110	3	1.4	12	5.0
110-120	33	15.9	46	19.1
>120	3	1.4	12	5.0
Total	207		241	

approximate a square, less often they are oval. The mean width: length ratio is 0.99 i.e. approaching 1. The distribution of specimens in classes of length and width is asymmetrical with one mode (length: 0.6-2.2 cm and width: 2.1-2.2 cm). The curve of thickness distribution is similar, with the mode of 0.4 cm (Table 13).

Blades, too, are predominantly without cortex (422 specimens). Among cortical blades lateral cortex is more frequent (62 specimens) than distal (26 specimens). This, too, confirms that cores in an advanced phase of preparation were used (Table 6-8).

Blades from single-platform cores outnumber considerably (396 specimens) those from double-platform cores (43 specimens). A relatively large number of trimming blades (67 specimens), both one- and two-sided, points to advanced preparation of flaking surfaces of cores.

Blade platforms are mainly formed by a single blow (106 specimens out of 264 blades have preserved platforms), linear, facetted, unprepared and dihedral platforms are less numerous (Table 11). The general structure of blade platforms is fairly different than that of flake platforms. In all likelihoood this is the effect of the frequent use of the operation of platform rejuvenation by detaching large flakes or tablets.

The differences between blades and flakes can also be seen in the features of percussion points: first of all blade percussion points are less well-marked, the ratio of prepared butt edges is higher in the case of blades and the lip is more frequently present on the ventral side. These features evidence that a punch was more often used to detach blades than it was in the case of flakes. Percussion methods may have been more carefully chosen for blade removal than during core preparation.

On the other hand, the fact should be stressed that in respect of the quantitative structure of platform angles no essential differences exist between flakes and blades, which is shown in the lower part of Table 12.

Morphological features of blades such as cross-section, shape and profile point to a careful modelling of core striking faces and a tendency towards standardization of blanks. As far as cross-sections are concerned the proportions of trapezoidal and triangular specimens are similar, whereas multifaceted and irregular specimens are few. Blades with parallel sides predominate in respect of shape, blades with irregular sides, convergent and divergent occupy a further position. As far as profiles are concerned the number of straight and convex specimens is more or less the same, twisted profiles are much fewer (Table 14).

Blade dimensions which do not give curves with a distinct mode are characteristic. The dominant values in the various classes of length and width frequencies are located within broad frameworks effacing modes (length: the range of 2.6 to 5.0 cm, width: the range of 0.7 to 1.6 cm). On the other hand, the curves are distinctly less asymmetrical in comparison to flakes because

Table 13

Flakes and Blades: dimensions

	Flakes	Blades
Length min	0.7	0.8
max	6.4	8.6
mean	2.41	3.28
st. dev.	1.04	1.21
Width min	0.6	0.2
max	6.1	4.5
mean	2.22	1.34
st. dev.	0.87	0.54
Thickness min	0.1	0.1
max	3.0	2.4
mean	0.55	0.37
st. dev.	0.39	0.22
Width/Lenght min	0.29	0.07
max	3.21	0.72
mean	0.99	0.40
st. dev.	0.38	0.10

Table 14

Blade morphology

	N	%
A. Shape: parallel-sided	252	49.2
convergent	74	14.4
divergent	47	9.2
irregular	139	27.2
Total	512	
B. Cross-section: trapezoidal	184	35.9
triangular	207	40.3
multifaceted	75	14.6
irregular	47	9.2
Total	513	
C. Profile: streight	240	46.8
convex	221	43.1
twisted	52	10.1
Total	513	

there are no distinctly long or broad specimens. Thickness curves have a distinctly unimodal character with the mode in the range from 0.3 to 0.4 cm.

When the mean dimensions of flakes and blades are compared (Table

Table 15

Blades fragmentation

	N	%
Distal	76	21.3
Distal and mesial	48	13.4
Mesial	111	31.1
Mesial and proximal	32	9.0
Proximal	90	25.2
Total	357	

13) it can be seen that blades are on average 1.1 cm longer, and 0.9 cm narrower than flakes. The mean blade thickness is 0.6 cm smaller than that of flakes.

As far as blade fragmentation is concerned the proportions of distal, mesial and proximal sections are more or less equal (Table 15). This situation suggests that fragmentation took place on the site, in the course of blade production or during use, possibly more often as an accidental rather than intentional process. The domination of simple breaking over pressure or striking as methods of dividing blades is in agreement with the above observations. Simple single breaking was registered on 158 specimens (in 71 cases: from the ventral to dorsal side, in 87 cases in the opposite direction) and on 49 double-truncated specimens. The blades was fragmented by striking on the ventral side in the case of 23 specimens, and by striking the dorsal side in the case of 35 specimens. The same method of blade fragmentation was used for 7 double-truncated blades (i.e. mesial fragments). A mixed method of fracturing and striking was used in the case of 34 mesial specimens.

7.5. Flake fragments and small flakes

This category is represented by finds smaller than 1.5 cm, and includes chips, flake fragments, indeterminate fragments except tools, bladelets and their fragments. Majority of the specimens are numerous indeterminate flake fragments (270 specimens i.e. more than 50%). Small flakes and chips are the next group of 178 specimens together. These are fine waste from coring and waste from tool retouching. The latter group numbers about 40 specimens although their undisputable identification causes some difficulties. A separate group consists of flake fragments with sections of crests on the dorsal side (17 specimens).

The remaining specimens in this category are pieces of artefacts fragmented as a result of burning and shutters.

Some few fragments of waste from the production of specific tool types are worth mentioning (e.g. a fragment of a burin spall, a flake from the rejuvenation of an end-scraper front).

Finally, it is interesting that in the group of small flake fragments represented in this category distal fragments dominate over proximal, and especially mesial parts.

7.6. Retouched tools

The general structure of retouched tools group is given in Table 16. The most numerous group are laterally retouched blades. which should be supplemented with bladelets with lateral microretouching. These two tool groups together number 89 specimens i.e. almost half of all the retouched tools. Backed bladelets are next in number (43 specimens). Another important feature of the quantitative structure of tools is a very small number of burins (only two specimens). End-scrapers dominate considerably over burins (19 specimens).

Table 16

Major tool groups

Tool groups	Radiolarite	Limno–quartzite	Flint	Quartzite	Total	%
1. End–scrapers	18	1	–	–	19	10.2
2. Burins	1	–	1	–	2	1.1
3. Perforators	4	–	–	–	4	2.1
4. Retouched truncations	10	–	–	–	10	5.4
5. Retouched blades	66	–	4	–	70	37.4
6. Backed bladelets	43	–	1	–	44	23.5
7. Retouched bladelets	20	–	–	–	20	10.7
8. Side–scrapers	3	–	–	–	3	1.6
9. Retouched flakes	7	–	–	–	7	3.7
10. Notched–denticulate tools	2	–	–	1	3	1.6
11. Blades strongly used	5	–	–	–	5	2.7
Total	179	1	6	1	187	
Burin spalls (>1.5 cm)	5	–	–	–	5	
Total	184	1	6	1	192	

The end-scraper group is represented by the following types:
— 2 simple blade end-scrapers (Pl. 1: 6; 2: 3),
— 3 end-scrapers on unilaterally retouched blades (Pl. 1: 5; 2: 1),
— 3 end-scrapers on bilaterally retouched blades (Pl. 1: 8, 9; 2: 2),
— 5 end-scrapers on partially retouched blades (Pl. 1: 1, 2, 3, 4, 7),
— a nosed end-scraper (Pl. 2: 1),
— a shouldered end-scraper (Pl. 2: 5),
— 5 flake end-scrapers: three specimens without marginal retouch (Pl. 2: 6, 8, 10), one with marginal retouch on one side (Pl. 2: 9), and a specimen with marginal retouch on both sides (Pl. 2: 7).

Burins are represented by only two specimens: a burin on an obliquely retouched truncation (damaged – Pl. 1: 3) and a transversal polyhedral burin on a flake (Pl. 3: 7).

There are four different types of perforators:
— a microperforator on a flake (Pl. 3: 4),
— a flake perforator with a broad point, inversally retouched in the proximal part (Pl. 3: 5),
— a microperforator on a bladelet; the broken point is obversally retouched (Pl. 3: 7),
— an atypical perforator (*bec*) on a blade (Pl. 3: 6).

There were 10 retouched truncations representing the following types:
— 4 obliquely retouched truncations on blades (Pl. 3: 9-11; 4: 1),
— 2 straight distal truncations on blades (Pl. 3: 12; 4: 5),
— an obliquely retouched proximal truncation on a blade (Pl. 4: 4),
— a convex distal truncation on a blade (P1. 4: 2),
— a straight proximal truncation on a blade (Pl. 4: 6),
— a microlithic proximal obliquely retouched truncation (Pl. 3: 13).

The biggest group of marginally retouched blades is represented by 69 simple specimens and a specimen with a retouched truncation (Pl. 4: 3). The specimens can be divided into four groups:
— unilaterally retouched blades (Pl. 4: 7, 9; 6: 6; 7: 1, 6; 8: 2, 4, 5, 8-14; 9: 1-8; 10-13, 15),
— bilaterally retouched blades (Pl. 4: 8; 5: 7, 9; 6: 1-3, 8, 9, 11; 7: 2, 5,7-8,11; 8: 1,3,6,15),
— pointed (*appointées*) blades (Pl. 4: 10; 5: 1-6,8,10,12; 6: 4,5,7; 7: 10,12; 9: 14),
— blades with Aurignacian-type retouch (Pl. 5: 11; 6: 10; 9: 9).

There were 16 complete backed blades and 27 fragments. The following types were represented:

— there was only one complete microgravette with an inversely retouched point and a rounded base (Pl.10: 1),
— two fragments may have belonged to the tips of such points (Pl. 10: 17,20),
— micropoints with obverse retouch on the edge opposite to the back (Pl. 10: 6,16),
— complete simple backed bladelets (Pl. 10: 5,7,8,11,12,18,25),
— nearly complete backed bladelets with obverse retouch on the opposite edge (Pl. 10: 10,13,14,15,28),
— mesial fragments of simple backed bladelets: with an obversely blunted back (Pl. 10: 31,32,33,34,39,42) and with an inversely blunted back (Pl. 10: 29,30,35).
— mesial fragments of backed bladelets with marginal retouch of the opposite edge (Pl. 10: 38,40),
— a proximal part of a simple backed bladelet (Pl. 10: 36),
— a distal fragment of a backed bladelet with marginal retouch of the opposite edge (Pl. 10: 37),
— a simple backed bladelet with an inversally retouched opposite edge (Pl. 10: 41),
— backed bladelets with a transversally retouched distal end (Pl. 10: 9,24,26),
— backed bladelets with a concave base obversally retouched (Pl. 10: 27),
— mesial fragments of a bilaterally retouched backed blade with pseudo-burin scars in the proximal end. These burin blows may have been the effect of using the bladelet as a projectile point, which was probably hafted when the blow was being struck and when the tip was broken. This specimen was brought to the site together with a wooden haft of the projectile arm (arrow?) in order to mount a new point in it (Pl. 10: 23),
— a fragment of an arched backed blade (Pl. 10: 19).

Bladelets with simple marginal retouch (smaller than 3 cm – larger specimens have been ascribed to the group of blades) are represented by 9 complete specimens and 11 fragments: – bilaterally retouched bladelets: obversely (Pl. 8: 7,11; Pl. 11: 5-10, 13-15,17,18) and alternately retouched (Pl. 11: 4), – unilaterally retouched specimens (Pl. 11: 3,16,19), – partially retouched in the distal part (Pl. 11: 2), – pointed bladelets (Pl. 11: 11).

Only three side-scrapers were discovered: two lateral (Pl.11: 21,22) and one transversal specimen (Pl. 11: 20).

There were 7 retouched flakes: laterally retouched (Pl. 12: 1, 4, 5, 7), with lateral-transversal retouch (Pl. 12: 2), and transversally (Pl. 12: 6) or bilaterally retouched (Pl. 12: 3).

Denticulated-notched tools are represented by two transversal specimens (Pl. 12: 8,10) and a lateral-transversal tool (Pl. 12: 9).

8. GROUND STONE TOOLS

Nine artefacts representing the category of grinding stones were discovered. The specimens were made from sandstone (6), quartz (1), quartz-pyroxene-chlorite shale (1) and indeterminate sedimentary rock (1).

The artefacts belong to the following functional groups:

— two retouchers from flat sandstone pebbles: one is small, oval (Pl. 13: 7), the other irregular, cracked transversally (Fig. 25: 3), On their flat side both specimens show wears such as striations and craters (lines and dots) caused by resting the worked lithic objects against the surface.

— a small, flat, round pebble with use wears round its circumference from functioning as a small hammer; this is also a sandstone pebble (Pl. 13: 6).

— edge hammerstone made from quartz flake core (Pl. 13: 8).

— two fragments of sandstone tablets with concave surfaces which functioned as lower grinding stone for crushing dyes or plant food. Both active surfaces are strongly polished, at places even glossy (Fig. 25: 1,2).

— a spindle-shaped object made from indeterminate sedimentary rock. It was worked by pecking over its whole surface. One tip is pointed, slightly asymmetrical, the other rounded (Fig. 25: 4), The function of this object is not known.

— a small cylindrical point with a conical tip (length of preserved fragment – 2.55 cm, diametre – 0.57-0.60 cm). The object is carefully polished although it was made from a very hard stone namely: quartz-pyroxene-chlorite shale (Fig. 25: 5). This was probably the tip of a drill; no microscopic traces of wear on the conical tip have been established which suggests that it was used for working in soft material e.g. as a drill for kindling fire.

This object was subjected to mineralogical-petrographical and use-wear examinations carried out by M. Pawlikowski. In order to indentify the raw material diffractometric analysis, qualitative X-ray analysis and fluorescent chemical analysis were used. Use-wear analyses were carried out using the scanning

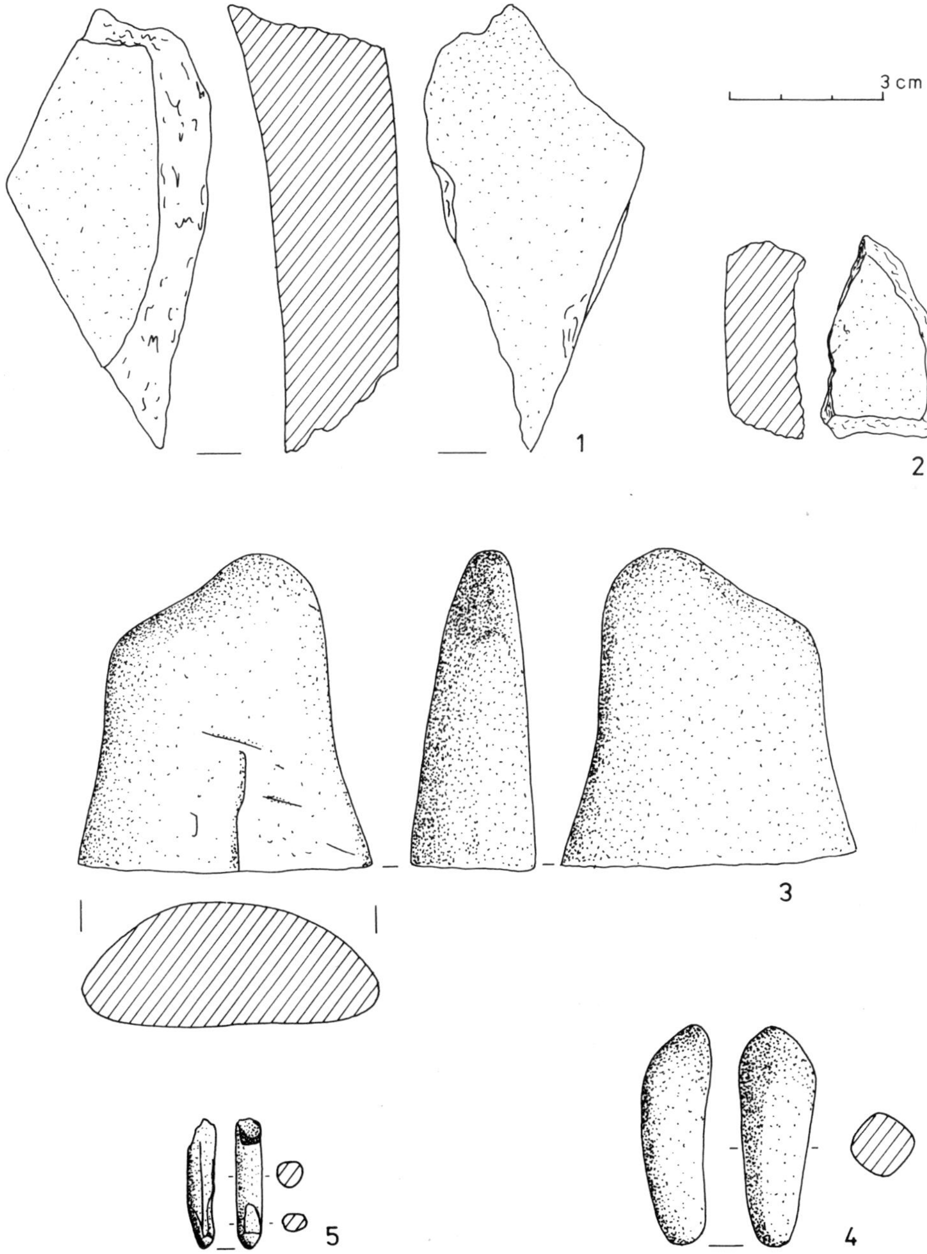

Fig. 25. Moravany-Žakovska. Ground stone implements.

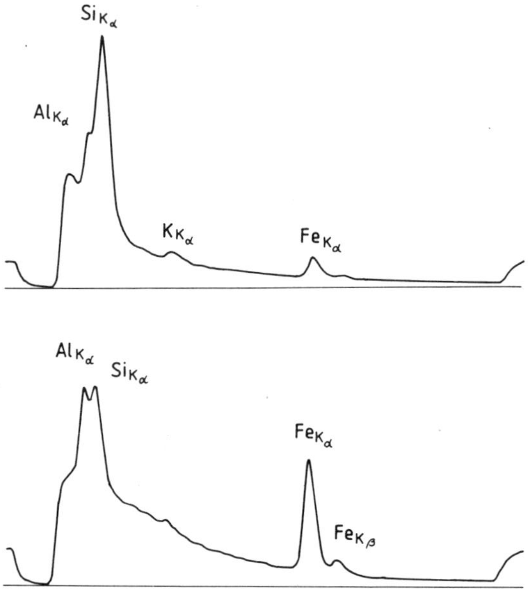

Fig. 26. Moravany-Žakovska. X-ray fluorescence pattern of a stone implement (see Fig. 25: 5).

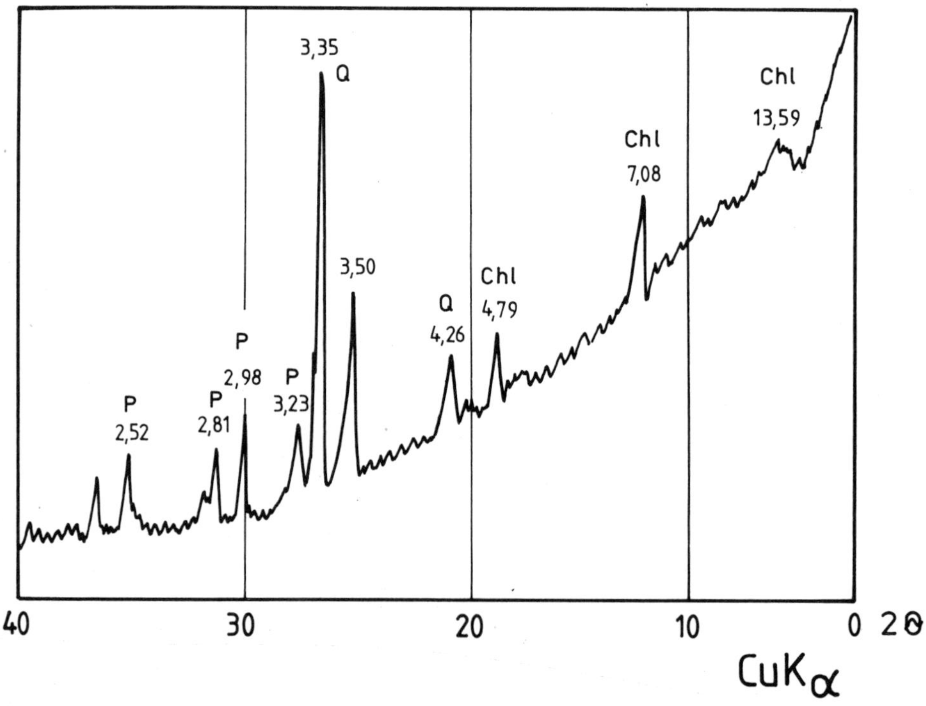

Fig. 27. Moravany-Žakovska. X-ray diffraction pattern of a stone implement (see Fig. 25: 5).

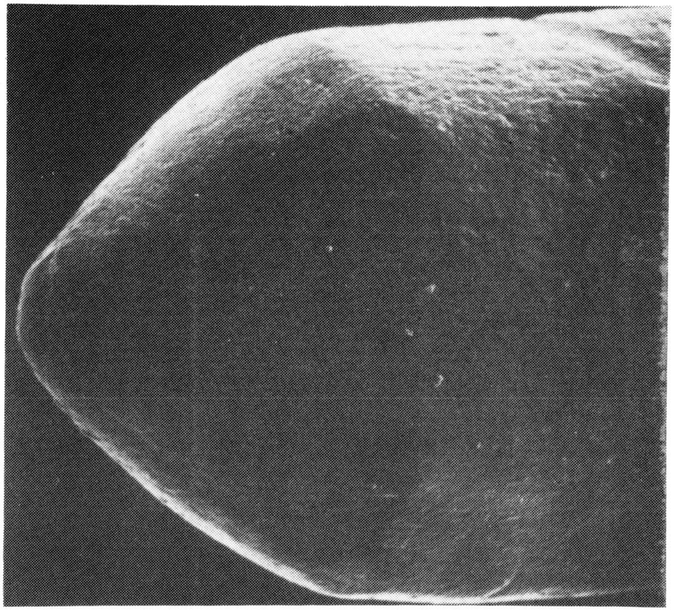

Fig. 28. Moravany-Žakovska. Conical tip of a stone implement as viewed in the SEM (20×).

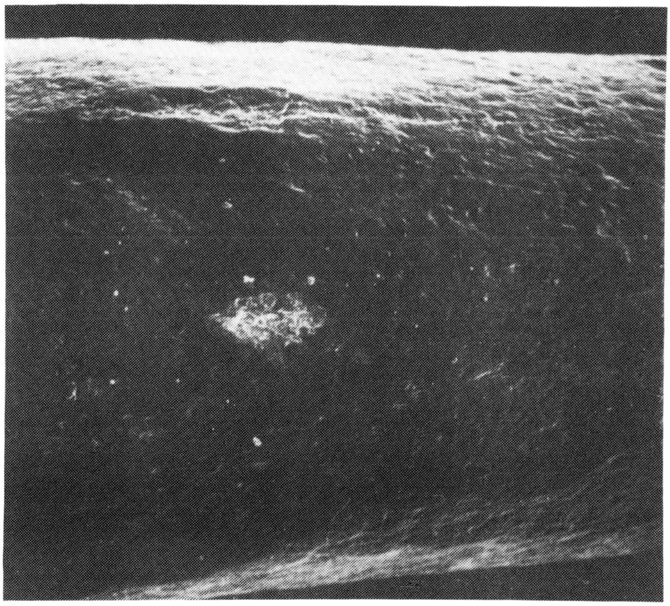

Fig. 29. Moravany-Žakovska. Fragment of the lateral surface of a cylindrical stone implement body with micro-basin (SEM – 20×)

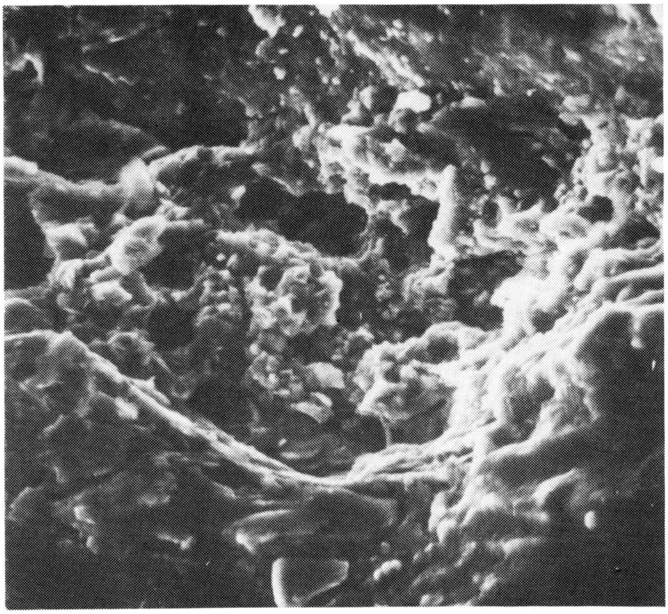

Fig. 30. Moravany-Žakovska. Inner surface of the micro-basin from Fig. 29 (SEM – 450×).

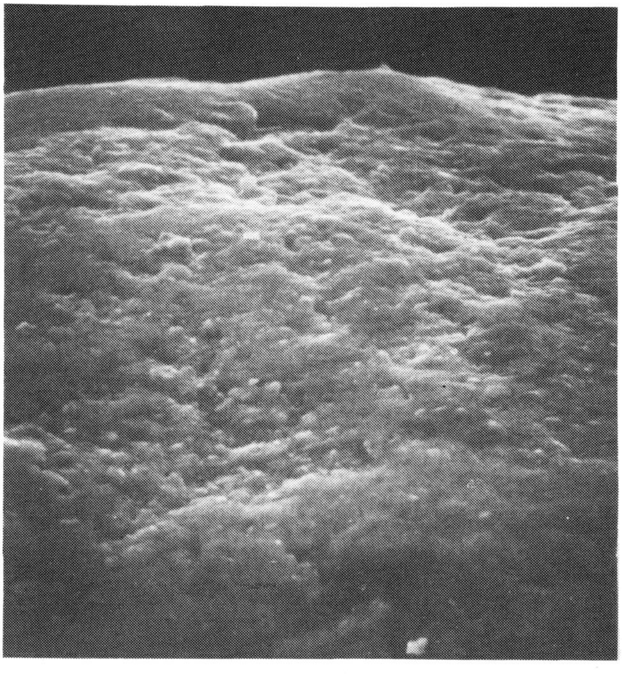

Fig. 31. Moravany-Žakovska. Fragment of the surface of conical tip of an implement (SEM – 110×).

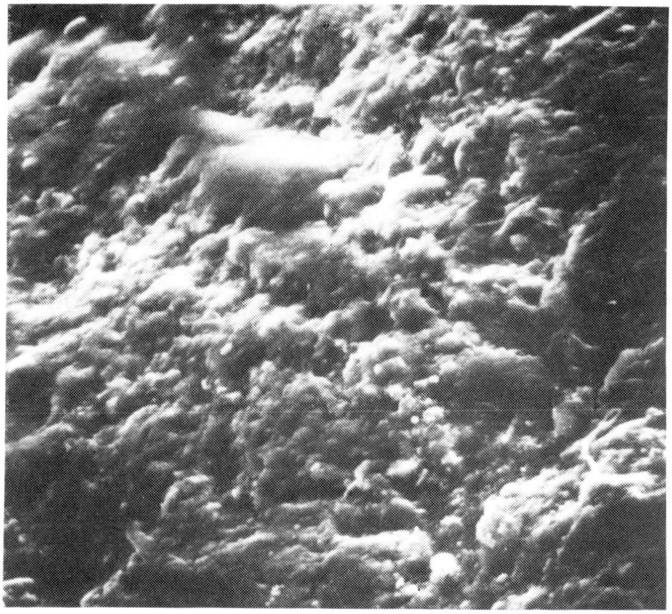

Fig. 32. Moravany-Žakovska. Fragment of the surface of conical tip of an implement SEM – 550×).

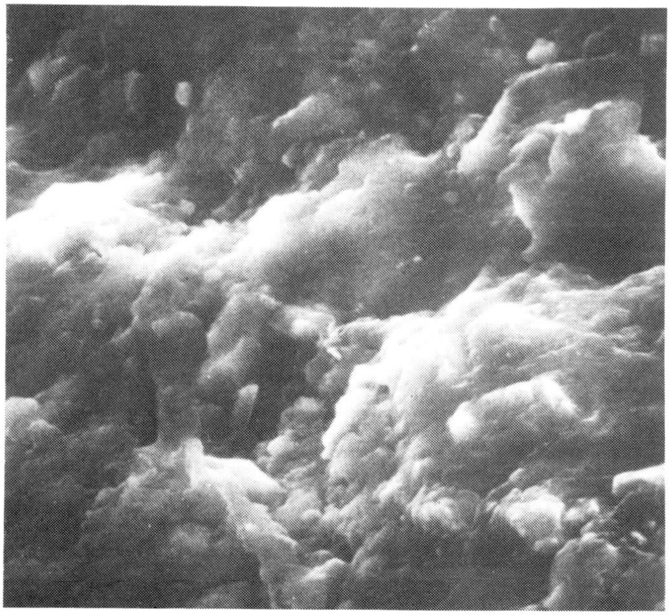

Fig. 33. Moravany-Žakovska. Fragment of the pointed tip of a stone implement (SEM – 2200×).

microscope. Diffractometer DRON 2 was used in the X-ray analysis. The powder method and monochromatic radiation of the cupric X-ray lamp were used. The results were interpreted using computer program XRAYAN.

Qualitative chemical analyses were made by means of a fluorescent X-ray attachement mounted on the scanning microscope. The analyses showed that the object under discussion contained mainly silica, aluminium, iron and small quantity of potassium (Fig. 26).

The X-ray diffraction of the natural surface of the object identified the material of which the object was made as metamorphic quartz-pyroxene-chlorite shale (Fig. 27). Similar rocks are known only from metamorphic massifs of which the closest are the Sudete Mountains.

Use-wear examinations have established that the conical tip of the tool was intentionally polished (Fig. 28), The outer surface is smooth. Occasionally on the lateral surfaces of the cylindrical body of the tool fine irregularities of the natural surface of the raw material can be seen (Fig. 29); the natural fine-grained structure of the raw material appears in the depressions (Fig. 30). Also in the proximal, fractured part of the object there are shallow basins (Fig. 31) which in larger magnifications reveal the structure of the raw material (Fig. 32, 33). Neither the conical tip nor the cylindrical body of the tool show linear wears from using the object. It can be assumed that after careful polishing the tool was used for perforating soft materials or possibly as a fire drill. These functions caused further smoothing of the tip and sides but did not leave linear traces on the hard raw material of which the tool is made.

9. MINERAL DYES

(by Maciej Pawlikowski and Joanna Trąbska)

In the course of the exploration of the site a total number of 64 fragments of various type haematite, 8 fragments of pink limestone, 7 limonite fragments and 8 pyrite fragments were discovered. All these raw materials could be used, especially after burning, as dyes. The total weight of all haematite fragments is more than 1 kg which should be supplemented with another kilogram from L. F. Zotz's investigations.

Mineralogical-petrographical analyses were performed for nine samples of various types of haematite and two limestone fragments (Table 18). The diffractometre X-ray analysis was made using DRON 2.5 diffractometre. The

Table 17

Analysed haematite samples from the site of Žakovska

Inventory number	Macroscopic characteristics
455	coarse-crystalline heamatite
432	medium-crystalline haematite with fine quartzite veins
754	medium-crystalline haematite
667	medium-crystalline haematite
757	fine-crystalline haematite fine-crystalline hematite
824	medium-crystalline haematite
254	sedimentary rock sandy limestone type
108	pink limestone
214	fine-crystalline haematite
277	medium-grained haematite

Table 18

Results of X-ray phase analyses of investigated haematites from the site of Žakovska
(mineral composition calculated with the accuracy of up to 5% of weight).

Inventory number	Main mineral	Accessory mineral
455	heamatite 50%	
	quartz 50%	
432	haematite 75%	quartz 25%
754	haematite 70%	quartz 30%
6E7	haematite 90%	quartz 10%
757	haematite 50%	
	quartz 50%	
	haematite 90%	quartz 10%
824	haematite 65%	quartz 35%
254	calcite 65%	quartz 30%
		hematite 5%
108	calcite 60%	hematite – trace quantity
	quartz 40%	
214	haematite 95,%	quartz 5%
277	haematite 9090%	quartz 10%

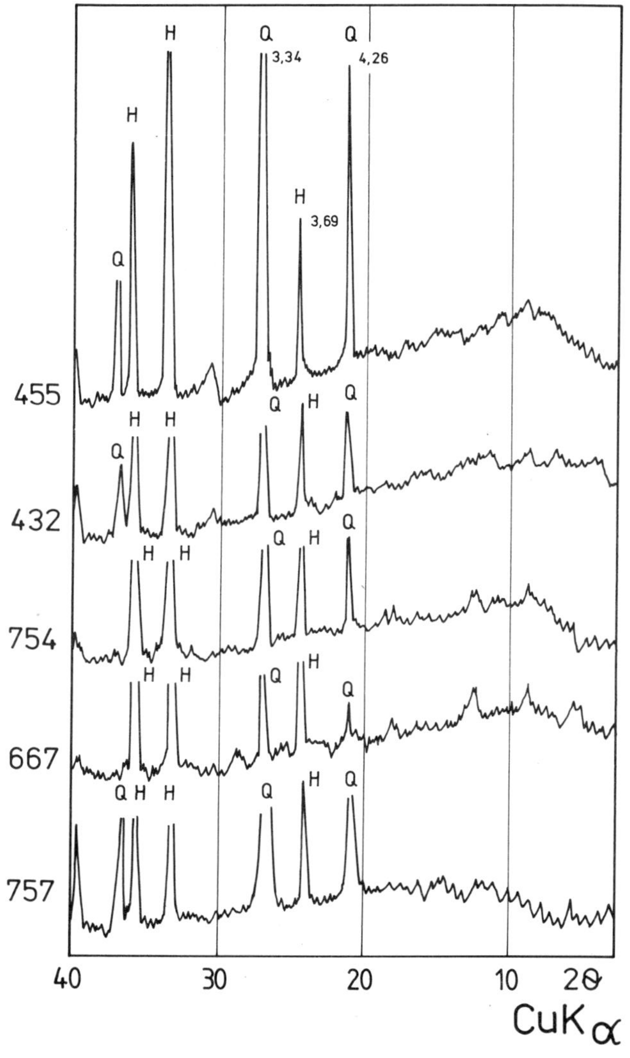

Fig. 34. Moravany-Žakovska. X-ray diffraction patterns of haematite samples.

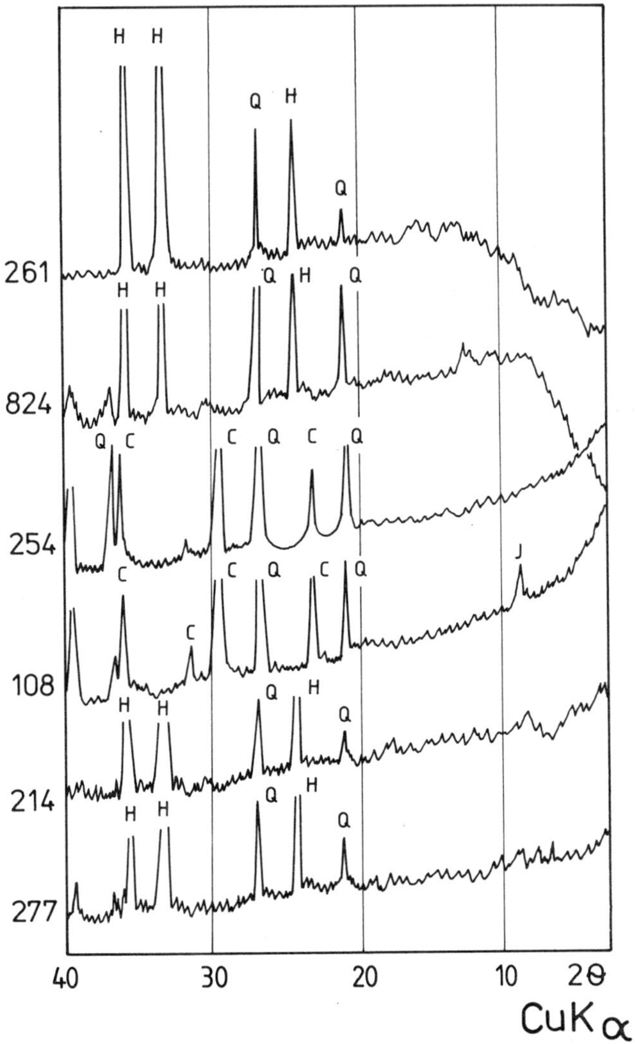

Fig. 35. Moravany-Žakovska. X-ray diffraction patterns of haematite samples.

powder method and monochromatic radiation of the X-ray cupric lamp were used. The results were interpreted using the XRAYAN computer program. The results are presented in Fig. 34 and in Table 18.

At the same time a field survey was carried out in order to identify haematites from haematite outcrops and the haematites discovered on the site. The ASA method was used in the chemical analysis of the haematites from the site. The following elements have been identified: Mn, Zn, Ni, Cu, Pb, Cr (Table 19).

Table 19

Trace elements content in haematite (%)
natural outcrops: I – sample from outcrop at Hubina, II – sample from the stream of Striebonica.

	Žakovska site		Natural outcrops	
	haematite I	haematite II	haematite I	haematite II
Mn	0.0110	0.0230	0.01110	0.0240
Zn	0.0033	0.0022	0.0029	0.0019
Ni	0.0062	0.0052	0.0059	0.0055
Cu	0.0045	0.0009	0.0040	0.0011
Pb	0.0033	0.0022	0.0030	0.0019
Cr	0.0120	0.0025	0.0100	0.0090

The results of analyses of haematites from outcrops and those from the site were compared using a computer program. The similarity of the two groups of haematites oscillates within the range of 50 to 67% with 100% indicating identical materials (Table 20).

Table 20

Similarity of haematites (in percentages) from natural outcrops near Moravany and haematites from the archaeological site of Žakovska.

Haematite from the site	Haematite from natural outcrops			
	sample no	CS-Mo-H1	CS-Mo-H2	CS-Mo-H3
	CS-Mo-H1	67	67	50
	CS-Mo-H2	67	67	50

9.1. Results of field survey

In the neighbourhood of the archaeological sites at Moravany haematite was found both within rocks such as dolostones, limestone conglomerates, bastard granite, and in the form of pebbles in the river Striebornica. Areas of ocurrence of haematite are marked on the map in fig. 36. Haematite is present in a variety of types.

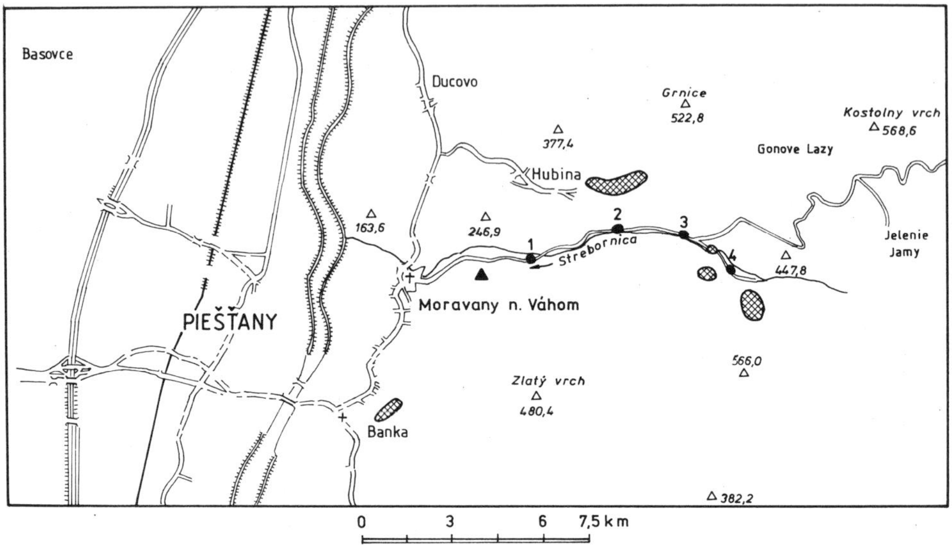

- haematite outcrops 1÷4 - samples from river alluvia

Fig. 36. Moravany. Locations of haematite outcrops and samples from river alluvia.

Haematite outcrop at the village of Hubina

The road through the village of Hubina (in the eastern direction) begins near a dolomite quarry of Slovita which in the west is topped by the Kostolec Mountain with remains of a protohistoric earthwork. The dolomite outcrop, cut with white veins, can be seen just behind the last buildings of Hubina on the left. Another outcrop is situated 15 metres further, also on the left. Here a small pit was dug in the soft, white, strongly desintegrated limestone rock cut with dense soft, yellow veins.

A hundred metres further an intentional outcrop was found just behind the last bus-stop in the village. It is about 6 m long and 2 m high. In the top part there is a thin layer of soil ranging from 0.1 to about 0.30 cm in thickness (Fig. 37). Haematite occurs here in lenses and veins running in the N-S direction, with a dip of about 30 degrees. The thickness of veins and lenses ranges from 10 cm to 1.5 m. The boundary lines with the surrounding rock are distinct. The matrix are light-grey dolostone and similar, hard and compact, usually fine-crystalline limestone. Sporadically, in the narrower zones in between the veins, limestone becomes brittle.

Numerous minerals in the form of efflorescence of various colours can be seen in the metamorphosed zones. Haematite occurs throughout the hill and is clearly distinguishable owing to its cherry colour. At the top of the hill outcrops of grey, non-calcareous silty shale occurs besides the limestones.

The described outcrop revealed several types of haematite co-occuring with other rocks, namely:

A) haematite-silty shale,
B) haematite-silty-calcareous shale,
C) limestone with a large haematite component,
D) brittle calcareous-haematite rock.

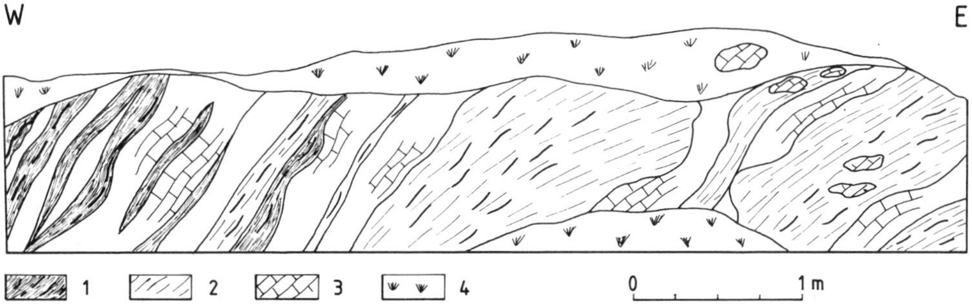

Fig. 37. Hubina. Profile of the outcrop: 1 – haematite shale, 2 – haematite veins, 3 – limestone, 4 – dolostone.

All the shale types are fairly easily crushed with fingers. They are dark cherry in colour with greyish tint. The limestone with the haematite component is also brittle, light cherry in colour. The last, brittle rock type is dark-grey-cherry in colour.

Natural outcrop in the vicinity of the Krahulče Skaly

The route to the Krahulče Skaly follows the Striebornica stream, then the green touristic route to the right and up the hill. Along the path various rocks are visible: granitoid rocks, siliceous rocks, cracked grey dolostone cut with white veinlets, and haematite whose thickness in the outcrop is about 3.5 m. Further along the path grey dolostone appears again. The top part of the hill i.e. the Krahulče Skaly is built of white limestones forming cliffs. Haematite is contained here in the soft haematite-silty shale which forms a fairly weathered surface eluvium. The rock is browncherry in colour.

Haematite in gneiss

Following the Striebornica stream in the direction of its sources, to the right just before the road forks, the path crosses the stream and climbs up wooded hillocks. They are built primarily from gneiss and granite-gneiss of various types. In these rocks haematite is dispersed as patch-like concentrations and veins sometimes parallel to the gneiss laminae.

Haematite in the Striebornica stream

In order to establish the presence of haematite pebbles in the Striebornica stream samples were obtained at four points in the stream at intervals of about 1 km from the foothills of the Moravany-Žakovska site to the sources of the stream. Axes a, b and c of the pebbles were measured. They were classified using Zinng's diagram, the degree of smoothing was visually evaluated. The pebbles were identified in terms of petrography.

At present the stream is used for fish farming. Haematite was found in the sediments of the stream at point 1 amounting to 3%. It is present as pebbles measuring 16-11-3, 16-12-2 and 13-8-5 cm (axes a, b, c respectively). These are pebbles of haematite-silty rock.

Sampling point 1

The sediments contained:

- granites (muscovite, muscovite-biotite, biotite, graphic and pegmatite type),
- gneiss (feldspar-quartz, biotite type),
- quartzites (grey, yellow, rusty),
- quartz (milky, dark grey, yellowish),
- dolostone (grey dolomicrite, veined),
- sandstone quartzites,
- shales and grey mudstones,
- haematite in the form of pebbles,
- recent calcitic sediments.

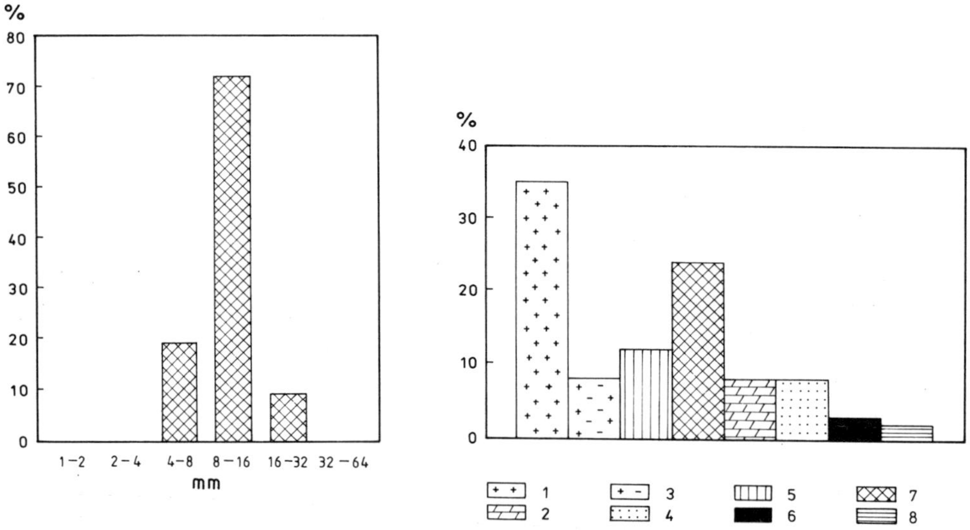

Fig. 38. Moravany. Sample 1 from alluvia of the Striebornica stream: left – granulometric composition, right – petrographic distributions (1 – granite, 2 – dolostone, 3 – gneiss, 4 – sandstone, 5 – quartzite, 6 – haematite, 7 – quartz, 8 – mudstone.

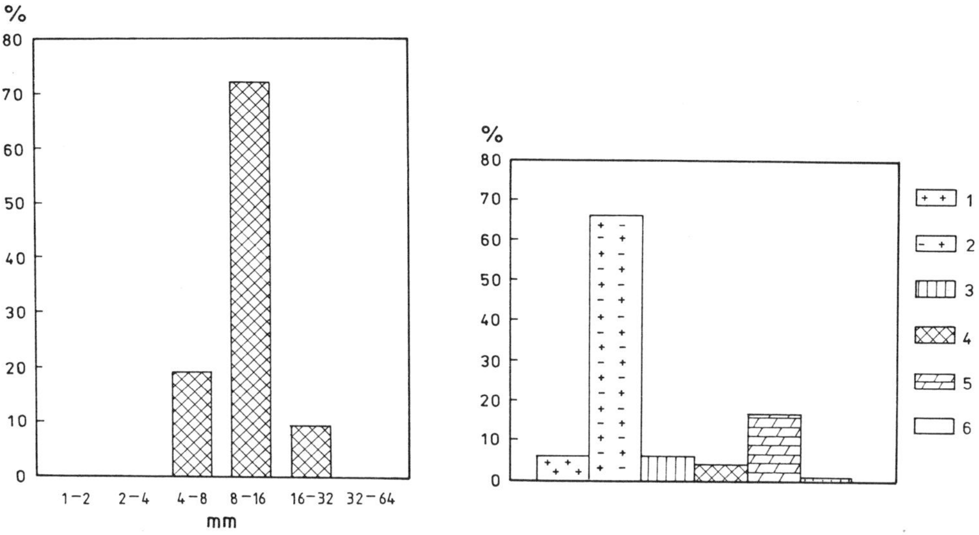

Fig. 39. Moravany. Sample 2 from alluvia of the Striebornica stream: left – granulometry, right – petrographic distributions (1 – granite 2 – gneiss, 3 – quartzite, 4 – quartz, 5 – dolostone, 6 – sandstone).

The results of petrographical analysis and the diagrams of the granulometric structure of samples is given in Fig. 38-41. Zinng's diagrams are presented in Fig. 42-44.

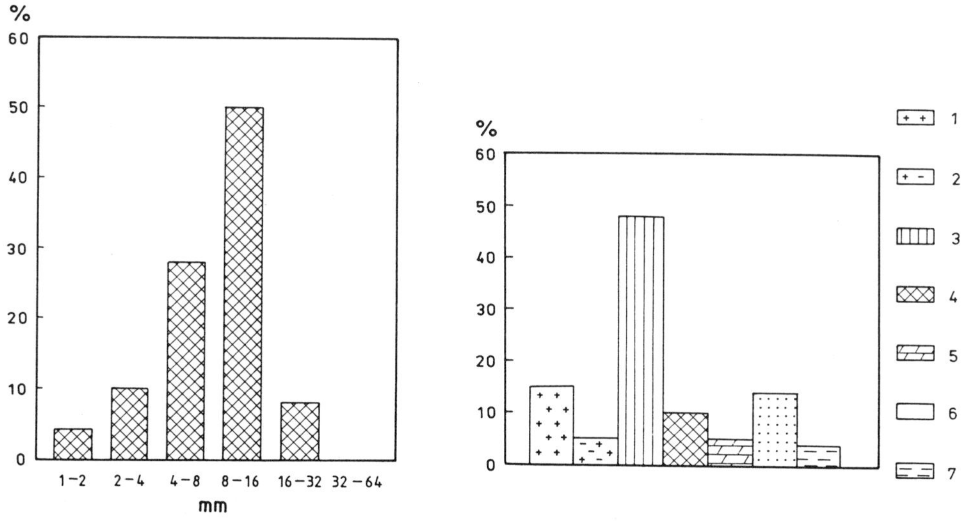

Fig. 40. Moravany. Sample 3 from alluvia of the Striebornica stream: left – granulometry, right – petrographic distributions (1 – granite, 2 – gneiss, 3 – calcite, 4 – quartz, 5 – dolostone, 6 – sandstone, 7 – shale).

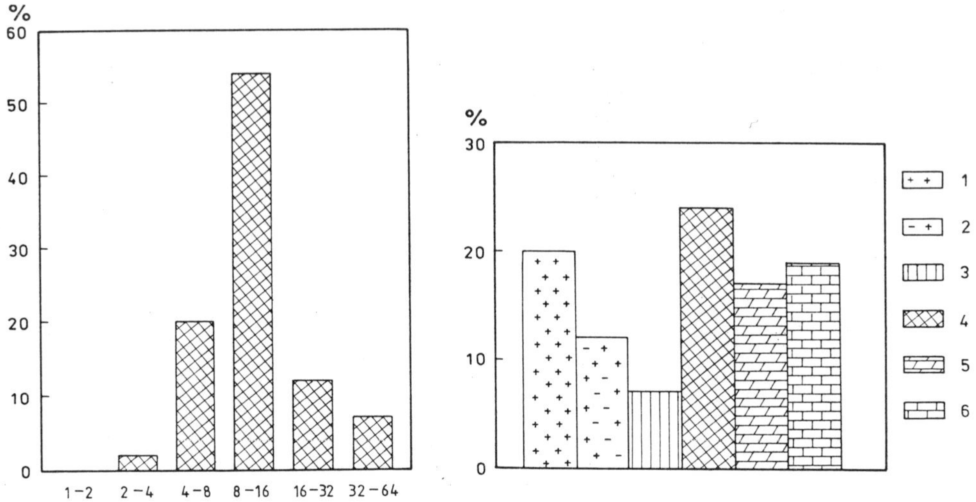

Fig. 41. Moravany. Sample 4 from alluvia of the Striebornica stream: left – granulometry, right – petrographic distributions (1 – granite, 2 – gneiss, 3 – quartzite, 4 – sandstone, 5 – dolostone, 6 – recent calcite).

In sample 1 granite (35%) is the dominant component of the petrographical composition followed by quartz and quartzite (24% and 12% respectively). Dolostone, quartzitic sandstone, gneiss, and mudstone occur in small quantities.

As far as grain size is concerned the fraction of 8 to 16 mm predominates, made up of weakly rounded pebbles and rough rock fragments. This observation

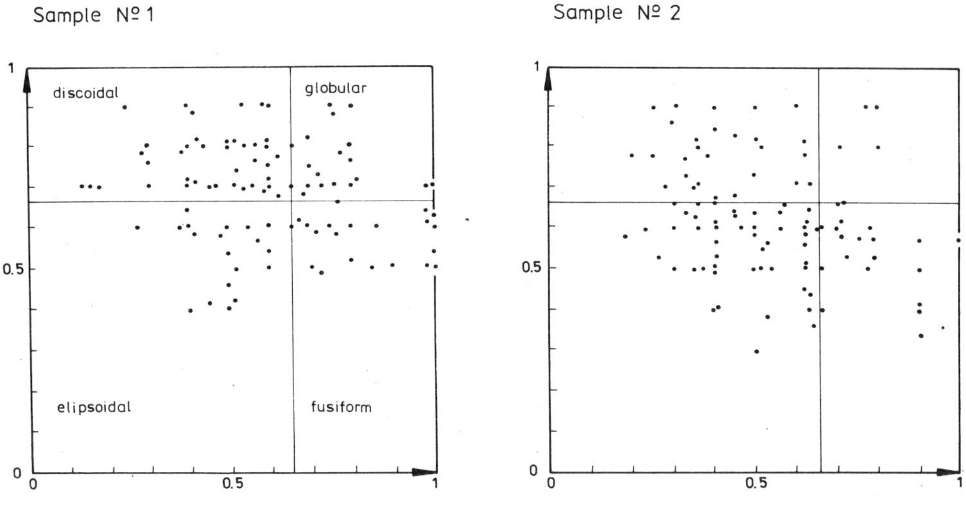

Fig. 42. Moravany. Samples 1-2 from alluvia of the Striebornica stream. Pebble typology acc.to Zingg.

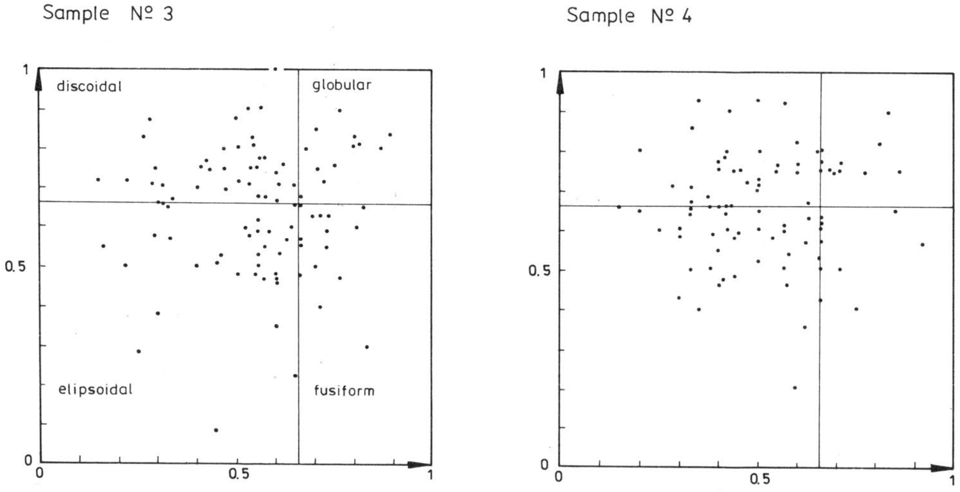

Fig. 43. Moravany. Samples 3-4 from alluvia of the Striebornica stream. Pebble typology acc. to Zingg.

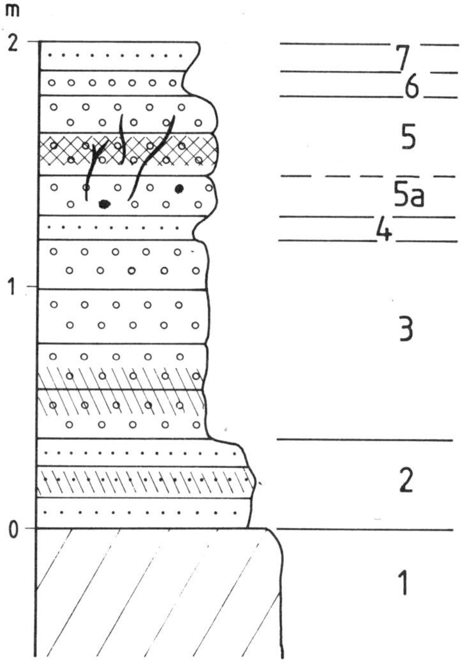

Fig. 44. Pieštłany-Banka. Profile of the bank of the river Váh: 1 – wall, 2 – variegated sandstone, silicified, with cherry-red mineralization zone, 3 – quartzitic breccia in ferrigineous--calcareous matrix, with cherry-red haematite mineralization zone, 4 – polymicritic sandstone in ferrigineous-calcareous matrix with secondary calcitic mineralization, 5 – quartzitic breccia in silty-siliceous matrix, showing secondary calcitic mineralization, silicified, 5a – layer of haematite pebbles, 6 – white quartzitic breccia with silty-siliceous matrix, 7 – white polimicritic sandstone with silty-calcareous matrix.

refers as well to other samples. The most numerous group are discoidal pebbles (40%); elipsoidal, fusiform (spindle-shaped) and spherical pebbles are 20% each group.

Sampling point no 2

Sample no 2 contains the biggest component of gneiss (66%). The biotite variety is dominant. Dolostone (17%) is a rock next in proportion. Other petrographical varieties do not reach 10%. These are: quartzite, quartz, sandstone and granite. The granulometric composition and the degree of rounding is analogous to sample 1. Pebble shape is predominantly elipsoidal (50%).

Sampling point no 3

Sample 3 contained the highest proportion of quartzite pebbles accounting for 48%. Next in respect to quantity are granite (18%) and sandstone (14%). Other rocks contained in the sample are dolomite and shale. Besides, quartz, originating probably from quartz veins, was also present. The grain size structure and degree of rounding as in the above mentioned samples. Pebbles are primarily discoidal (47%) in shape.

Sampling point no 4

Sample no 4 is dominated by quartz (24%) followed by granite (21%), and lastly by recent calcitic formations (19%). Pebbles are elipsoidal (46%) or discoidal (40%).

The outcrop near the Váh river

The outcrop in question is situated on the Hlohovec-Nitra road, at the bridge carrying the traffic to and from Piešt'iany, on the black tourist path. This is an outcrop of breccia with a zone of haematite and ochre mineralization. The outcrop is about 6 m long, and about 2 m high (Fig. 45).

The outcrop revealed the following rocks in the direction from the bottom to the top:

– variegated sandstones, polymicritic with various grain size, with fairly powdery, silty-ferruginous-siliceous matrix. This bed measures about 0.4 m in thickness. Within the bed there is a light cherry-coloured zone of weak haematite mineralization measuring several cm in thickness.

– conglomerates, primarily quartz conglomerates with fairly powdery iron-siliceous-carbonate matrix. The rock is variegated (rusty, red, yellow).

Within these beds, whose total thickness is about 1.5 m, a zone of strong haematite mineralization is contained. This zone is from several cm to about 0.5 m wide. Its intensive cherry-red colour is conspicuous. Haematite constitutes the matrix of conglomerate.

In the top part the conglomerate beds are intercalated with polymicritic sandstone, rusty in colour, with brittle ferruginous-calcitic matrix, with secondary calcitic mineralization. In the top part of the bed the conglomerates contain quartz pebbles; grain size ranges from several tenth to 3 cm along a axis. The matrix is silty-siliceous, white in colour. Secondary calcitic and siliceous mineralization can be seen in the form of veins and glazing. In this part of the outcrop a yellow silification zone, about 15 cm thick, can be seen.

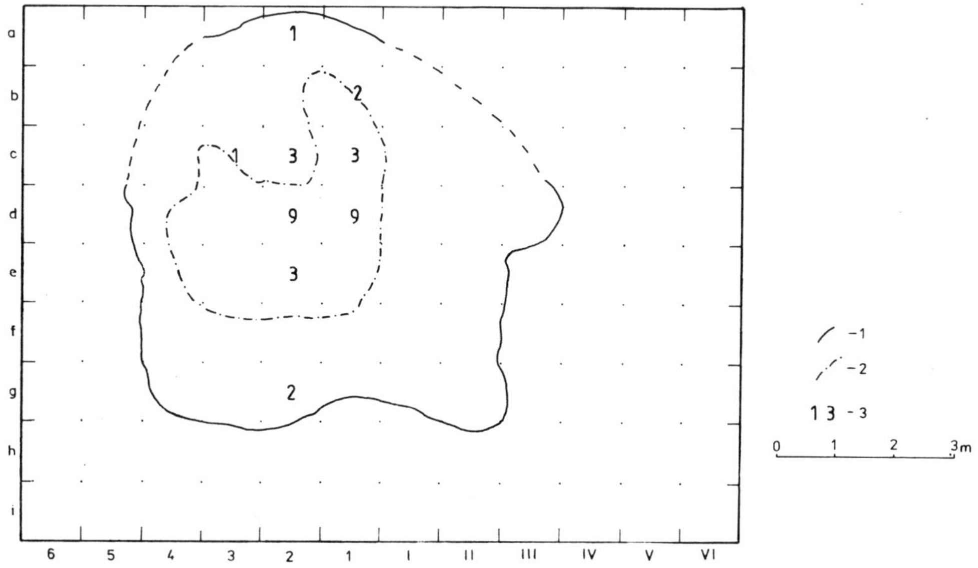

Fig. 45. Moravany-Žakovska. Horizontal distribution of charcoals: 1 – concentration of finds in level I, 2 – concentration of finds in level II, 3 – number and location of charcoal samples.

Particular beds of the conglomerate have various resistance which is clearly seen in the relief of the profile. In the upper part of the bed some few haematite pebbles were found, well rounded, oval, about 1.5 cm in size.

The profile is topped with polymicritic sandstone with silty-siliceous-calcite matrix about 15 cm thick.

Higher up the outcrop is overgrown and unavailable for observation. While climbing the mountain with the above-described profile, beds of white quartz conglomerates with brittle silty-siliceous-calcite matrix were observed.

9.2. Conclusions

The haematite in natural outcrops in the western slope of the Považski Inovec massif accompanies petrographically varied rocks and occurs in the form of pebbles in the Striebonica stream. There are different types of haematite: plastic silty, concrete shale, and haematite matrix of conglomerates.

Similarity of the haematite from the site of Žakovska with the haematites from outcrops within 7-8 km radius from the site was evaluated. This similarity was estimated on the basis of Fe content measured using ASA method and interpreted using a computer program. Analysis has shown that the similarity of haematites from the site and from natural outcrops oscillates within the range from 50 to 67%. Taking into account the high variability of haematites from natural outcrops this indicates with high degree of probability the exploitation of local haematite deposits.

10. RADIOCARBON DATING (by Anna Pazdur)

The date was obtained on charcoals. They were usually coated in loess and came from square cl, from a depth corresponding to the second chronological horizon (50-55 cm). As a preliminary preparation the samples were washed with the 2% HCl solution. Further preparation of samples and measuring procedures were carried out in accordance with the standard methods used in the C-14 Laboratory at Gliwice. The obtained date is:

Gd-4915 **18 100±350 years B.P.**

11. ANTHRACOLOGICAL ANALYSIS
(by Maria Lityńska-Zając)

In the course of field work 35 charcoal samples were obtained from several squares in order to perform botanical analyses. Their position was two-dimensional. Most samples come from the areas where flint material from the two distinguished settlement phases ocurred. For this reason charcoal samples should be treated together: as originating both from the lower and the upper occupational level. Samples from squares a2 and g2 were connected only with the older phase. Charcoals were present in 33 samples. Part of this material, namely 61 charcoals were identified, part was used for radiocarbon dating. The charcoals were first sorted out under a binocular lense with the magnification of 25. The crosssections of the fresh break were examined. Attempts at preparing anatomical samples failed in several cases. For this reason the material was identified on three fresh planes namely: transversal, radial and tangenital using a stereoscopic microscope with up to 250 magnification. In other cases microscope slides were prepared and charcoals were identified.

Generally, the charcoals were very small, the maximum size being 0.5 cm. Their structure was weakly preserved and they were highly friable. Part of the material (19 fragments) could not be identified because of poor preservation.

On the basis of well preserved charcoals pine – *Pinus sylvestris* and yew-tree – *Taxus baccata* were identified. The poorly preserved charcoals were ascribed to indeterminate conifers – *Coniferae* indet. The taxonomic composition of charcoals from particular squares is given in Table 21.

Table 21

Results of antthracological analysis

Square/Taxon	No of sample/Number of charcoals								
a2	1								
Pinus sylvestris	1								
b1	1	2							
Taxus baccata		2							
indet.	1								
c1	1	2	3						
Coniferae indet.		1							
indet.	1		6						
c2	1	2	3						
Pinus sylvestris		1	1						
indet.	1								
c3	1								
Coniferae indet.	2								
d1	1	2	3	4	5	6	7	8	9
Pinus sylvestris	1			1			1		2
Taxus baccata			2		3				
indet.		1				1		1	
d2	1	2	3	4	5	6	7	8	9
Pinus sylvestris			4			1		2	6
Taxus baccata							1		
Coniferae indet.	5	2					1		
indet.			1	1					
e2	1	2	3						
Pinus sylvestris		1							
indet.	2		2						
g2	1	2							
Pinus sylvestris		1							
indet.	I								

Description of identified charcoals

Pinus sylvestris L. – common pine – On the transversal plane rows of tracheids can be seen; those closer to the centre have larger aperture and are thin-walled. Younger elements, on the outer surface have smaller aperture and are thick-walled. Resin canale are present. On the radial plane, in the cross-field the outer cells of the pith ray have undulating walls with funnel-shaped pits. The inner rows of pith rays have larger window-like pits.

Taxus baccata L. – common yew – On the transversal plane the boundaries between annual growth rings are distinctly visible. There are no resin canals. On the tangenital plane there occur high pith rays. On the radial plane in the cross-field tracheids do not occur. Rows of pith rays cell can be seen with characteristic cavities. The tracheid walls show distinct spirals.

Discussion of results

The quantitative and qualitative composition of charcoals preserved on the site at Moravany is very poor. The charcoals were present in nine out of the squares demarcated on the site. The biggest number of charcoals has been preserved in squares d2, dl and c1. In other squares only individual specimens occurred. Quantitative differences and percentages of proportion between the various texons are given in Table 22.

Pine has been preserved in biggest quantities and was present in the biggest number of saemples on the site. The second taxon, namely yew-tree, was present in three samples numbering a total of eight fragments. It should be added that

Table 22

Number and ratio of particular species

	Square									
Number of samples	a2	bl	cl	c2	c3	dl	d2	e2	G2	Total	1%
	1	2	3	3	1	9	9	3	2	33	
Species	Number of charcoals in samples										
Pinus sylvestris	1			2		5	13	1	1	23	38
Taxus baccata		2				5	1			8	13
Coniferae indet.			1		2		8			11	18
indet.		1	7	1		3	2	4	1	19	31
Total	1	3	8	3	2	13	24	5	2	61	100

considering the small number of discovered charcoals and small taxonomic differentiation the proportions of various taxons are fairly accidental.

The discovery of yew in the material is of great importance. At present common yew grows mainly in central and southern Europe in the oceanic climatic zone (Środoń 1975). The eastern boundary of its range runs to the east of the Riga Bay, across Lithuania, the eastern part of Poland, through the Białowieża Forest, in the region of Chełm and Roztocze. Then the boundary of yew runs between Przemyśl and Lwów across the Eastern Carpathians. The northern boundary of yew runs across Scandinavia reaching as far as 63° of northern latitude. In the south yew occurs as far as the Caucasus, in Asia Minor, Crimea, Algeria, Spain. Yew is present in Madeira and the Azores (Tomanek 1987).

Yew is a shade-loving tree growing, especially when young, under the canopy of other tree-tops. As to temperature yew is fairly demanding. It is sensitive to frost and in dry, exposed areas it can easily get frozen. Yew requires fresh, moist soils with a high water-table (Białobok, Hellwig 1955; Pokorny 1967). It can grow both on soils rich in alkaline compounds as well as on acid soils, However, the most favourable conditions for yew are provided by fertile, humic clay-sandy or clayey soils (Bugała 1975). Yew-tree stands occur at about 1450 m a.s.l. in the Carpathians (Król 1975).

The Quaternary history of yew reflected in pollen diagrams suggests that its occurrence is related to warm climatic oscillations. At present yew is known from many Holocene flora sites and from all interglacial periods (Srodoń 1975). It is also found as macroscopic remains in the warmest phases of interglacial periods when mixed forests with alder developed. In the younger phases of the two last interglacial periods yew persists for a long time. It is present even at the end of the interglacial when pine-birch forests become more important and a change to cool and wet climate can be observed (Środoń 1975).

The presence of yew on the site of Moravany-Žakovska, whose dating suggests the end of Pleniglacial II maximum, is curious. On the same site there were other finds of yew. Charcoals of *Taxus baccata* were discovered during excavations in 1949 (Ambrož *et al.* 1952). Yew-tree occurred as well on other palaeolithic sites in Slovakia (Table 23, Hajnalova, Krippel 1984) and on fossile soil sites e.g. in the travertines from Ganovce (Kneblova 1960). Its occurrence was unquestionably established during interglacial periods. Yew was identified also at Dolni Vestonice II (Moravia) dated at 26 390±270 b.p. (ISGS 1744) that is at Pleniglacial II (Mason *et al.* 1994).

During Pleniglacial II "secondary climatic oscillations and slightly warmer episodes can be observed at about 23.000 and 17.000 years" (Starkel 1983). It is likely that in favourable climatic and landscape conditions, on the edges of of mountains, clusters of these coniferous trees could have survived (Starkel 1983; Mamakowa, Starkel 1977). Warmer climatic oscillations were recorded

Fig. 46. Moravany-Žakovska. Charcoals of *Taxus baccata* (left – transversal section, right – radial section.

in the pollen diagram of Smerek II site in the Bieszczady Mountains (south-eastern Poland) where pollen of trees such as *Picea, Pinus cembra* and *Pinus silvestris,* of heliophilous bushes such as *Salix, Juniperus, Hippophaë and Betula nana,* and pollen of herbs were identified. These spectra have been dated at 16 950±325

Table 23

Charcoals of *Taxus baccata* from Palaeolithic sites in Slovakia

Site	Dating	Other species represented
Piešťany-Banka	R/W; W	*Fagus sylvatica*
Piešťany-Banka II	R/W; W	*Fagus sylvatica, Pinus* sp.
Nove Mesto-Mnešice	R; R/W; W	*Pinus* sp.
Moravany-Dlhá	W inpgl.	*Pinus mugo, Pinus* sp., *Acer* sp., *Alnus* sp., *Betula* sp., *Laburnum* sp., *Viburnum* sp.
Moravany-Žakovská	W pgl. II	*Larix* sp., *Picea* sp., *Pinus* sp.

(R – Riss, W – Würm, R/W – Interglacial Riss/Würm, inpgl. – Interpleniglacial, pgl. – Pleniglacial)

years BP. One of the interpretations offered by the author of pollen analysis was the possibility of the occurrence of an interstadial oscillation between 16.000 and 18.000 BP (Ralska-Jasiewiczowa 1980), Some of the pollen diagrams in Europe from that period confirmed the appearance of flora which could be interpreted as interstadial (Ralska-Jasiewiczowa 1980 and literature quoted in the same work). However, none of the diagrams in question provided evidence of distinct amelioration of climate which would make the growth of yew possible.

The explanation of the discovery of yew at the site of Moravany-Žakovska is difficult and doubtful. It is possible that in the period in question there existed local conditions which enabled the survival of yew at relic sites. In the case of Moravany-Žakovska site conditions like this may have been provided by thermal springs located south-west of the site at a distance of about 5 km. The springs may have created a specific microclimate with milder conditions during the cold periods. If the conditions are favourable in respect of wetness yew may survive sometimes even cold, continental winters (Srodoń 1975).

Another explanation of the occurrence of yew at Moravany-Žakovska is that its was intentionally brought to the site because of useful properties of wood of this type.

Analyses of more charcoal samples and pollen diagrams will enable us to resolve these questions unequivocally.

12. THE FAUNA WITH *ARIANTA ARBUSTORUM* (L.)
(by Stefan W. Alexandrowicz)

Two species of molluscs have been found in ten samples of loess. As the material accessible to malacological analysis was washed during archaeological field work on sieves with the mesh size of 2.0 mm, only shells and fragments of shells of large snails remained in the residuum while specimens of small species had been completely lost. *Arianta arbustorum* (Linnaeus) occurs in all samples and *Trichia hispida* (Linnaeus) in three of them. Additionally an apex of *Pupilla* sp. was found in one sample. Although the molluscan assemblage in question is incomplete, some suggestions about the ancient environment can be presented.

Arianta arbustorum (L.) is a species living in different types of habitats, in damp places of both shady and open areas, in deciduous forests, bushes, hedgerows, meadows, mountain glades, epilithic grasslands and slopes covered with rock debris (mainly with limestones). Populations inhabiting lowlands comprise relatively large specimens contrary to mountain populations characterized by a considerable content of relatively small specimens. The last mentioned are described from Alps and distinguished as *Arianta arbustorum alpicola* (Ferussac). This taxon prefers sunny or only partly shady places and seems to be connected with severe climatic conditions (Klemm 1973, Baur 1984). Similar shells of *Arianta arbustorum* (L.) described as forma *alpicola* or forma *minuta* characterize a cold climate as components of both recent and pleistocene molluscan assemblages (Geyer 1927, Jaeckel 1962).

Arianta arbustorum (L.) has been found in many profiles of loess and loess-like deposits (Ložek 1964, 1965, Alexandrowicz 1987, 1988, 1991). Subfossil shells from these sediments are relatively small and correspond to those of the mountain populations. They occur in relatively rich assemblages and are accompanied with: *Trichia hispida* (L.), *Pupilla muscorum* (L.), *Succinea oblonga elongata* (Sand.), *Vallonia tenuilabris* (Braun) and *Clausilia dubia* Drap. as well as with *Pupilla loessica* Lož., *Semilimax kotulai* (West.), *Lymnaea truncatula* (Müller) and shells of slugs (Ložek 1964, 1965, Alexandrowicz 1988, 1991). Such an assemblage is typical of cold but not extremely cold intervals of a glaciation. In the Cracow Region and in the Pieniny Mts. it occurs in loess of the Vistulian age as an indicator of the last interpleniglacial. In the locality of Maszków near Cracow shells of *Arianta arbustorum* (L.) from loess enriched in slope detritus (slopewash) were dated with the radiocarbon method on 23.900 ± 850 years BP, Gd–4123 (Alexandrowicz 1991).

The fauna with *Arianta arbustorum* (L.) and *Trichia hispida* (L.) from the archaeological site of Žakovska can be compared with related assemblages from loess and loess-like deposits described in the South Poland. It indicates a fairly wet, open or poorly shady habitat with a dense vegetation as well as climatic conditions corresponding to the interpleniglacial of the Upper Vistulian.

13. REMAINS OF FOSSIL MAMMALS
(by Henryk Kubiak)

The site of Moravany nad Váhom-Žakovska contained a large number of very small fractures of animal bones.

All the bones are of similar yellowish-brownish colour, generally badly preserved. Most of them are crumbled into very small pieces. Many of the pieces are covered with calcitic precipitations.

The excavated bone material consists of fractures of limb bones, skulls, probably vertebrae and ribs, jaws and single remains of teeth.

Among 126 samples examined, only in 14 of them determinable bone and teeth fragments could be found. Those remains belong certainly to three species of mammals, i.e. the woolly mammoth (*Mammuthus primigenius*), reindeer (*Rangifer tarandus*), roe deer (*Capreolus capreolus*), and probably red deer (*Cervus elaphus*) – one piece of an antler.

Except for mammal bones, no remains of other animals were found at the site. Actually the majority of the bone fragments are not determinable, and therefore neither human and animal activities on the bone material nor abnormalities in the teeth and limb bones could be found. Such characters are possible to be recognized on better preserved and less crumbled bone material.

The bone material is now deposited in the Institute of Archaeology of the Slovak Academy of Sciences.

Material and remarks

Woolly mammoth – *Mammuthus primigenius* (Blumenbach)

Among the numerous bone fractures of the site described fragments of teeth, bones of the skull, pieces of limb bones and pelvis are represented. There are two pieces of an alveolus of a tusk, i.e. parts of a skull (samples 3, 5) which could be recognised. In samples 16 and 32 small pieces of lamellae of molar teeth could be determined.

Other small pieces of strongly crumbled bones probably belong to mammoth remains too. Those were present in following samples: 1, 2 (pelvis ?), 4, 40, 52, 55, 64, 87, 88, and samples: "b 2 group E", Pr. c. 1077/92 a2", "group D", "b 2".

Reindeer – *Rangifer tarandus* (Linnaeus)

There were: one right calcaneus (sample 46), one phalanx III of the right posterior limb (sample 60), two pieces of an astragalus (probably from the same animal) (sample 60), one knee cap (patella) (sample 80), one distal fragment of a femur (sample 15), and teeth: P_3, M_1 of the left part of the lower jaw (sample 54), M_2 of the left part of a lower jaw (sample 92), the left half of an upper jaw with P_2, M_1-M_3, (sample "group E, e3"), the left part of a lower jaw with M_2-M_3 (sample "group E, e/3"), and one fragment of a right scapula (sample "group E, e/3").

Besides determinable teeth and bone fragments there were also small pieces of bones belonging probably to reindeer: samples – 31, 42, 59, 51, 90, and "Pr. c. 1078/92 a 3", "d 2",

Bones and antlers of reindeer are known from nearly all parts of Europe in notably increasing abundance to the north. However, the systematic position of the Pleistocene reindeer in Europe is still uncertain (Kubiak 1987). Thus far the reindeer remains from the site described are referred also to *Rangifer tarandus*.

Roe deer – *Capreolus capreolus* (Linnaeus)

Two single incisors were found – samples: "d/I, sonda 4/91, 25-40 cm", "1/4, 45-50 cm".

After Davis (I987) the roe deer together with the extinct straight-tusked elephant (*Palaeoloxodon antiquus*), the extinct woodland rhino (*Dicerorhinus mercki*), the hippo (*Hippopotamus amphibius*), wild boar, fallow and roe deer usually characterise faunal assemblages from the last interglacial period. The same author mentions the presence of roe deer among other species of large herbivorous mammals whose in herds were clearly abounded in Hoxnian Britain.

In this way it shall be suggested that the roe deer occurred usually in interglacial periods, contrary to the cold-adapted woolly mammoth and the reindeer mentioned above.

Red deer – *Cervus elaphus* (Linnaeus)

One small piece of an antler was found (sample 19). Although the determination of this piece is not certain it seems to belong to this species.

Wolverine – *Gulo gulo* (Linnaeus)

Only one, fortunately well preserved, second phalanx of the second toe of the right hind limb could be found. Comparative studies seem to show that this smal bone belongs to this species.

The wolverine is known from Upper Palaeolithic sites of Europe. Its recent distribution ranges from northern parts of Europe, Asia, to North America. It occurs in forests as well as in tundra.

General comments

The remains of the woolly mammoth and the reindeer, predominating in this site, are well known as typical tundra animals aasociated with open treeless areas – they indicate a tundra-steppe under cold conditions.

The roe deer and the red deer, however, are animals connected with the forest, and their occurrence in the past seems to show milder thermal conditions (interglacials), although the Pleistocene mammal species seem to have shown a great tolerance in relation to temperature conditions.

Seasonality of site occupation

Faunal indicators of seasonality at Moravany are more than few. Among the material studied there are two deciduous molars (Fig. 47: 2), from an animal retaining these molars at the time of death. These molars have high relief wear

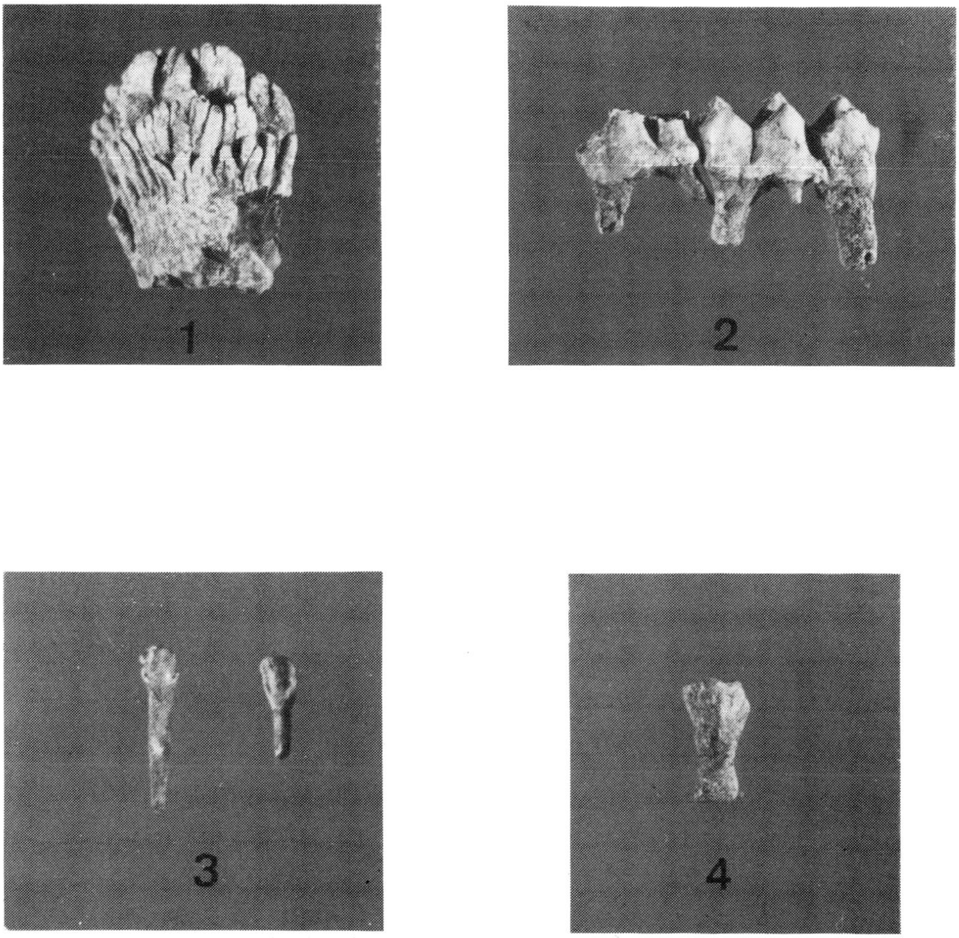

Fig. 47. Moravany-Žakovska.

1. *Mammuthus primigenius*(woolly mammoth), fragment of molar tooth (sample 32).
2. *Rangifer tarandus* (reindeer), buccal view of teeth less than two years old. The high relief wear patterns of the teeth in this example indicate death sometime during the first to seventh month (i.e., mid-June to mid-December) (sample 54).
3. *Capreolus capreolus* (roe deer), incisors (samples d/I, 1/4).
4. *Gulo gulo* (wolverine), phalanx (sample 77).

Fig. 48. Moravany-Žakovska.
5. *Cervus elaphus* (red deer), fragment of an antler (sample 19).
6. *Rangifer tarandus* (reindeer), calcaneus (sample 46).
7. *Rangifer tarandus* (reindeer), phalanx (sample 60).

patterns suggesting this event occurred sometime during the animal's first through seventh months of life. This would place the time of site occupation sometime between mid-June to mid-December.

On the other hand while the phalanx and the calcaneus (Fig. 48: 6,7), were not splintered for marrow, it may be considered that the inhabitants of the site were not forced to rely on food sources necessary during colder months of the year.

14. DISCUSSION AND CONCLUSIONS

Our investigations into the site of Moravany-Žakovska have finally enabled us to close the discussion about the age and taxonomic position of this site. Since the publication of investigations from the year 1949 (Ambrož *et al.* 1952) this site has been often ascribed to the Aurignacian, notably to the Krems group. This view may be supported by some morphological features of cores and scrapers on the site and the presence of finely retouched bladelets.

However, recent investigations have yielded typical gravettian elements and provided the radiocarbon date of 18 100±350 (Gd–4915). This date places the Žakovska site unquestionably at the beginning of the post-Pleniglacial period. This has enabled us to ascribe the site to the Epigravettian (as defined by J. K. Kozłowski, 1986 p. 133) as an example of the post-Pleniglacial phase of the middle European industries with backed blades and bladelets.

In the local Upper Palaeolithic sequence known from several tens of find-spots in the region of Moravany and Banka the Žakovska site represents, therefore, the final phase of palaeolithic settlement which followed:

1. industries with Moravany-Dlha type leaf-points (Bárta 1960), probably from the end of the Interpleniglacial (on the other hand as there are no dates a possibility of their later age cannot be excluded if only on the grounds of the chronological position of similar points at Trenčianskie Bohuslavice – Bárta 1989).

2. Gravettian industries with shouldered points representing the type known first of all from Moravany-Podkovica (Barta 1970). Taking into account the date from Nitra-Čermaň (22 860±40; GrN-2249) and the recently obtained date from Moravany-Lopata (21 410±610; Gd-9246) it can be assumed that the *pointes à cran* horizon corresponds to the period from 23.000 to 21 000 years B.P.

On the basis of the present knowledge of materials from other sites in the Moravany complex we can say that no other site is known that would represent this precisely, late post-Pleniglacial settlement phase. It should be added that radiometric determinations for archaeological sites from the period from 20.000 to 15.000 years B.P. are rare in the whole of the middle Danube basin, despite the fact that recent investigations have supplied several important discoveries. Table 24 provides a list of radiometric dates obtained from palaeolithic sites in the territories of Slovakia, Moravia, Lower Austria and Hungary from the period between 20.000 and 15.000 years B. P. These sites, at the same time, describe the circle of analogies both taxonomic and behavioral that we are trying to find for the site of Žakovska.

Table 24

Radiocarbon dates for Epigravettian sites from the period 20 000 – 18 000 years B.P. in the Middle Danube basin

Nr.	Site	Country	Lab no	B.P.
1	Stranska Skala IV	Moravia	GrN-13945	18 220±120
2	Sagvar upper layer	Hungary (Transdanubia)	GrN-4038	17 760±350
3	Stranska Skala IV	Moravia	GrN-14351	17 740± 90
4	Moravany-Žakovska	Western Slovakia	Gd-4915	18 100±350
5	Grubgraben AH3+4	Lower Austria	Lv-1660	18 700±300
6	Grubgraben AH4	Lower Austria	Lv-1680	18 400±300
7	Jászefelsőszentgyörgy	Hungary (Alföld)	Deb-1647	18 500±400
8	Kašov upper layer	Eastern Slovakia	Gd-6569	18 600±390
9	Arka lower layer	Hungary (Upper Theiss basin)	A518	18 700±190
10	Madaras	Hungary (Upper Theiss basin)	Hv-1619	18 805±405
11	Sagvar lower layer	Hungary (Transdanubia)	Grn-1783	18 900±100
12	Grubgraben AH4	Lower Austria	AA-1746	18 960±290
13	Mogyorósbánya	Hungary (Transdanubia)	Deb-1169	19 930±300

Geological framework indicates that despite considerable reduction of the profile of the Žakovska site due to later erosion, the culture levels are located at the boundary of two loess series, or – more precisely – within the lowest part of the youngest series. In this part of the youngest loess series thin intercalations of typical aeolian loess are separated by levels of washing-out. Here quartz grains rounded by slopewashing or of eluvial origin are present in greater proportions. All these components bear witness to variability of climatic conditions notably of humidity. It is interesting that occupational episodes are connected with the beginning or end of wetter phases and not with the aeolian sedimentation of loess.

Palaeomalacogical data, regretfully incomplete (the meshes of sieves for wet-sieving were too large), showed the presence of molluscs typical of open landscape but with some bushes such as *Arianta arbustorum* (acc. to S.A.

Alexandrowicz), Paucity of arboreal species represented only by *Pinus sylvestris* also points to fairly cold climatic conditions. On the other hand, the presence of yew (*Taxus baccata*) contradicts this interpretation. A possibility that yew was brought to the site intentionally (e. g. for the production of bows) cannot be excluded. Yew may have been brought from the more southern regions of Central Europe or from nearby refugia in the area of hot springs near Piešťany. Because yew needs shade provided by the canopy of other tree-tops then yew-tree refugia near Piešt'iany would have required larger forested territories.

That larger forest refugia existed not far away from Moravany is corroborated by the occurrence of deer and roe-deer in the fauna of the site of Žakovska. The strong contrast in respect of ecological requirements of tundra species such as mammoth and reindeer (dominant species) and forest species such as deer and roe-deer is a parallel of the contrast between ecological requirements of pine and yew. If the possibility of later contamination of faunal remains and charcoals is ruled out then we can hypothetically assume the existence of forest refuge areas near Piešt'iany as the effect of a variety of microclimatic factors and the presence of hot springs. It should be emphasized that neither typical forest species in the fauna nor sthenothermal species in the vegetation were found at other sites in the middle Danube basin in the period from 19.000 to 17.000 B.P.

Generally, the chronological and lithostratgraphical position of the Žakovska site is similar to the Grubgraben site near Krems in Lower Austria (Montet-White *ed.* 1990). Four out o five culture levels (nos 2-5) at Grubgraben are located at the boundary between two loess series: stratified and unstratified corresponding to initial or embryonic soil horizons. Level IV is dated at 18.400±330 and 18.960± 600 years B.P. (Haesaerts 1990, p. 31). Haesaerts maintains that initial soils developed during humid episodes of which two (HH1 and HH2) facilitated development of humic layers. In all likelihood these episodes belong to the Sagvar oscillation documented by pedological processes in the territory of Transdanubia. On the Sagvar site near Siófok on Lake Balaton they were dated at between 18.900±100 and 17.760±350 years B.P. These dates approximate the Laugerie-Lascaux oscillations in western Europe (A. Leroi-Gourhan 1980).

The profile at Moravany-Žakovska has shown that the site was occuppied four times in a relatively short time-span. Levels III-IV represent short occupational episodes. The first episode (level IV) can be seen as traces of a hearth, (burnt quartz, charcoals) and scattered fine bone fragments. The second episode (level III), besides traces of a hearth, left behind fine chips and pieces of radiolarite registered as few macrofinds and more numerous specimens in the fraction of less than 1 mm. Both occupational episodes were very short, probably one night, with a small group of palaeolithic hunters.

Two younger episodes (the radiocarbon date of 18.100±350, Gd-4915 refers to level II) are much more clearly observable as the accumulation of artefacts,

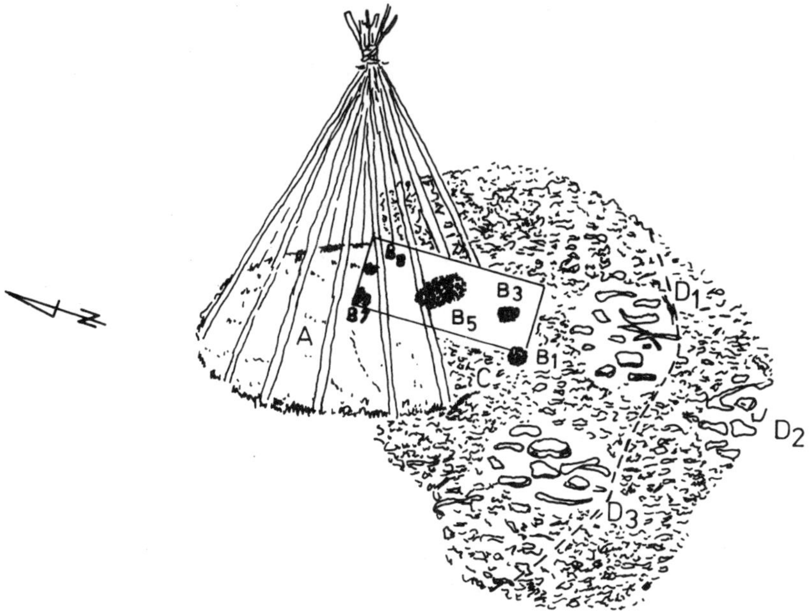

Fig. 49. Moravany-Žakovska. Reconstruction of light dwelling from level II. A – "zone de repos", B1, B3, B5, B7, B8 – "zones de combustion" recorded in the microfraction (see Fig. 21, 22), G – "zone intérieure d'activités domestiques", D – "zones de rejet" (concentrations of bones – D1-3).

bones, mineral dyes and traces of fire (burnt quartz, charcoals etc). Although the structure of the two camps is different it is characteristic that neither of the two levels (I and II) shows tendency towards spatial organization based on functional specialization. The scatter of debitage, all types of retouched tools, products from tool retrimming or resharpening are homogeneous within a concentration. On the other hand, the shape of each concentration is different. In level I it is crescent-shaped, distinctly asymmetrical in relation to the empty area where – hypothetically – a light tent may have been located (Fig. 49). In level I the concentration forms a compact, sub-circular "khshemenitsa".Thus, the situation in level II resembles structures typical of the Magdalenian from the Paris Basin, notably the single tent from Section 36 (A. Leroi-Gorhan, Brezillon 1972) where the location and existence of a tent was not documented by evident traces but by the asymmetry of artefact scatter in relation to the empty area. The situation in level I approximates more closely "kshemenitsa" type structures of the Late Paleolithic in the European Lowland where frequently the location of the hearth and the tent are not known, except for the hypothesis that the whole concentration of this type was protected by the tent wall or a wind-break (Schild 1984, p. 228). This hypothesis would contradict the concept of concentric zonality of camps of the primitive hunters justified in the works of A. Leroi-Gourhan (1976) and L. Binford (1980).

The differences in the sequence of the four occupational episodes, probably chronologically very close, concern first of all the permanence (duration) of occupation of the site during a given episode; there are no differences in respect of functional specialization. Differences of this kind occur at Grubgraben between five occupational events, which are chronologically close to the Žakovska site. Functional variability is manifested in the following characteristic features of particular levels:

AL 4 – dense accumulation of finds, hearths, predominantly butchering zones and thrash middens,
AL 3 – a typical butchering zone,
AL 2 – a typical domestic unit with a carefully laid pavement,
AL 1 – a workshop zone on the edge of the campsite.

Functional differentiation can be seen in the various concentrations of "kshemenitsa" type in the upper level of the epigravettian site Kašov in eastern Slovakia (Bánesz *et al.* 1992). This level has been dated to within a similar time framework namely: the beginning of the post-Pleniglacial (18.600±390 years B.P.). About a hundred concentrations, all situated on the same surface (due to slow rate of sedimentation and domination of erosional processes) were discovered. The concentrations show different composition in respect of major technological groups and tool categories. Among them concentrations such as: domestic units, workshops shaping cores, workshops producing blades etc. can be distinguished. However, all the concentrations are small, containing a relatively small number of artefacts which suggests short occupational events.

Finally, we should mention other examples of functional specialization in the period which is the object of our interest e.g. the butchering site Stranska skala IV in southern Moravia, dated at 18.220±120 and 17.740±80 B.P. (Svoboda 1994, p. 161).

In the light of the above remarks we can see that the Žakovska site parallels settlement pattern found in the Middle Danubian Epigravettian in the short duration of occupation which was caused by the greater mobility of population groups. However, the Žakovska site has not revealed the pattern of spatial-temporal division of activities performed on the sites. This may suggest that the social structure characterized by seasonal functional splitting of groups or generating more permanent specializations within the group did not extend in the whole of the Epigravettian. On the other hand, the important and more widespread phenomenon was the diminishing of group size to nuclear or less often extended family in comparison to pre-Pleniglacial Gravettian groups. In the latter groups seasonal aggregation into bigger units probably took place. These groups inhabited large settlements of the Pavlovian in Moravia and Lower Austria.

The assemblage from the Žakovska site differs from the pre-Pleniglacial

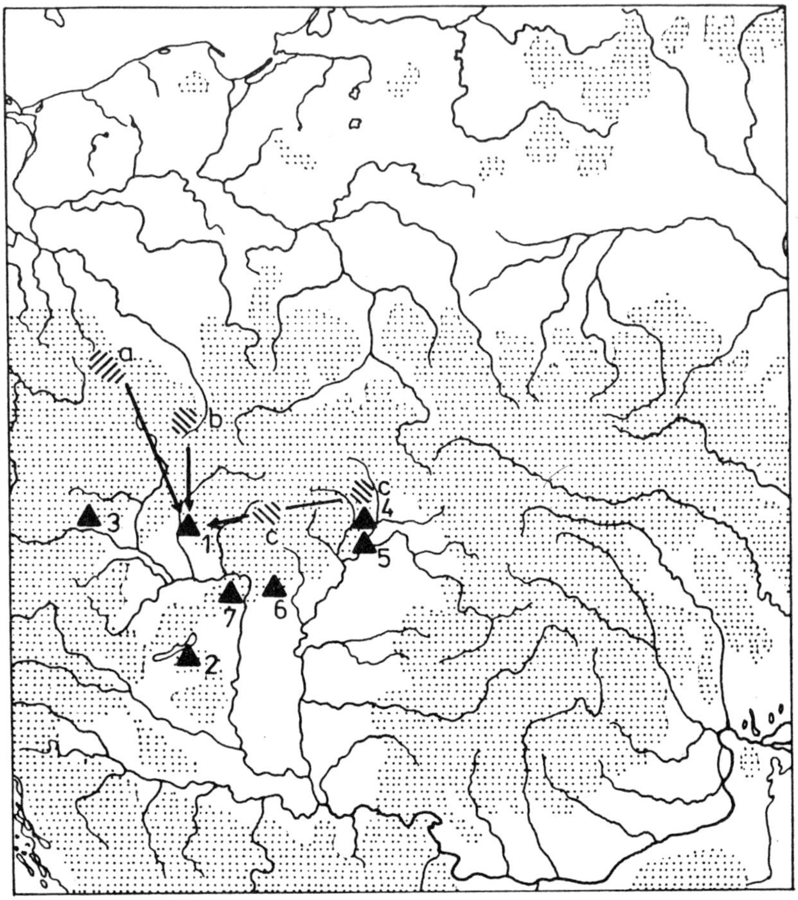

Fig. 50. Extralocal raw material sources: a – quartz-piroxene-chlorite shale from Sudetes, b – erratic flint from Upper Silesia, c – possible sources of limnoquartzites. Main epigravettian sites in the middle Danube basin: 1 – Moravany-Žakovska, 2 – Sagvar, 3 – Grubgraben, 4 – Cejkov, 5 – Kašov, 6 – Jászfelsöszentgörgy, 7 – Mogyorósbánya.

Gravettian, also locally represented in the region of Moravany by shouldered points industries, in having a much more clearly local system of raw materials procurement. While in the Gravettian assemblages from Moravany-Podkovica, Moravany-Lopata, Banka-Kňazevica, Banka-Kopanica and others the proportion of southern Polish flints is dominant (reaching as much as 80-90%) at Žakovska, on the other hand, local radiolarites predominate collected mainly from the alluvia of the Váh river. Altogether the proportion of radiolarites amounts to 94.6%. Other raw materials used in the chipped and ground stone industry are also partially local. The meso– and extralocal raw material component (Fig. 50) is represented by the following:

1. limnoquartzites – 0.9% – represented by flakes, blades, tools, and chips (without cores). These limnoquartzites may have come from central Slovakia from the area around Stara Kremnicka, or from eastern Slovakia from the region of the Slanske Mountains between the Torysa and Topl'a (see: Kaminska 1991), The deposits were situated at a distance of 100 km or 250 km away.

2. white patinated flints – 1.3% – are represented by similar technological groups (without cores). These flints are of southern Polish provenance, although without mineralogical and geochemical analyses it is difficult to establish whether this is erratic flint from Upper Silesian moraines or jurassic flint from the Kraków – Częstochowa Jurassic Plateau. The proportion of this flint is small. A hypothesis that artefacts made from it come from the processing of chunks or cores imported by pre-Pleniglacial Gravettian people for example from the neighbouring site of Podkovica, cannot be excluded.

3. quartz-pyroxene-chlorite shale from which the point-drill is made comes probably from the Sudetes from a distance of about 200-250 km away.

Thus, the system of procurement of lithic raw materials and mineral dyes is based on sources within 5 km radius from the site, mainly the alluvia of the river Váh and the Striebornica stream. Only 2-3% of raw materials comes from a distance of 100-250 km away, in the eastern and north-western direction.

In comparison to the pre-Pleniglacial Gravettian when the system of raw materials procurement along the south-north axis predominated (J. K. Kozłowski 1986a, p. 78), in the Epigravettian not only local raw materials predominate but the axis of contacts changes from meridional to latitudinal (J. K. Kozłowski 1994).

When Epigravettian lithic inventories from the middle Danube basin are compared (Table 25) it can be seen that indices of major tool groups reveal conisedrable variability. Features in common are: domination of end-scrapers over burins, a large component of blades with marginal retouch, and the mean index of backed blades from 17 to 23%, with the exception of the upper level at the Kašov site where this index is less than 2%.

The question can, then, be posed: into what taxonomic units can Epigravettian inventories from between 19.000 and 17.000 B.P. be divided? In the middle Danube basin and the Theiss basin these inventories show a number of specific features which are not so much indices of major tool groups frequency but rather some morphological features of these groups. On the sites such Žakovska and Kašov (upper level) the end-scraper group is characterized by a higher proportion of simple blade end-scrapers or end-scrapers on retouched blades. The transdanubian sites (Sagvar, Mogyorósbánya – Gábori 1959, 1964, Dobosi 1992, fig. 5: 1-6) and Grubgraben in Lower Austria (Montet-White *ed.* 1990) have typically a higher proportion of short or even sub-circular end-scrapers. All the epigravettian sites contain some number of end-scrapers with high fronts or even sub-carenoidal. This is the situation at Žakovska (Pl. 2: 1, 3), Grubgraben

Table 25

Major tool group structure in some Epigravettian (19000 – 18000 years B.P.) sites in the Middle Danube basin

Major tool group	Moravany-Žakovska (18000±340)	Grubgraben AH4 (18400±330)	Kašov upper layer (18600±390)	
			Concentrations 1-30	Total
End-scrapers	10.2	36.2	43.9	31.6
Burins	1.1	15.6	23.1	32.3
Perforators	2.1	3.2	1.7	2.3
Retouched truncations	5.4	4.5	0.9	1.3
Retouched blades	37.4	5.8	9.6	14.8
Backed bladelets	23.5	19.5	0.5	1.6
Finely retouched bladelets	10.7	*	0.9	0.8
Side-scrapers	1.6	–	2.0	1.6
Retouched flakes	3.7	–	4.3	n.c
Denticulated and notched implements	1.6	–	0.9	3.1
Splintered (scaled) pieces	–	10.4	0.5	0.7
Combined tools	–	–	3.8	n.c.

*) counted with backed bladelets
n. c. not counted.

(Montet-White *ed.* 1990 fig. IX-9: J,M,Q) and Kašov (Bánesz *et al.* 1992, Pl. 3: 18, 23, 35; 5: 9, 32; 6: 13), also Stranska skala IV (Svoboda 1994, fig. 76:3).

In the group of retouched blade specimens with rich, frequently multiseriate or even scaled retouches are typically present. Such specimens, resembling aurignacian *lames retouchées*, are known from the Žakovska site (Pl. 7:12; 8:14, 15) also as *appointé* blades (Pl. 5: 1, 3, 5, 6, 12). Analogous specimens occur at Grubgraben (Montet-White *ed.* 1990, Pl. IX-13: T) but they do not occur at Kašov or Sagvar.

In the group of backed bladelet the small ratio of typical microgravettes is characteristic. They were replaced by simple backed bladelets, truncated and backed bladelets and double backed bladelets. At the Žakovska site all these categories were fairly numerous (simple backed bladelets – Pl. 10: 5, 6, 11-15, 25; truncated bladelets – Pl. 10: 9, 24, 27, double backed bladelets – Pl. 10: 6, 17, 20). At Grubgraben there were simple and truncated specimens (Montet-White *ed.* 1990, Pl. IX-13: A-H), whereas at Sagvar there occurred first of all simple backed bladelets (Gábori 1959). At the site of Kašov –

upper level backed bladelets are very few, represented mainly by simple straight backed bladelets (Bánesz *et al.* 1992, Pl. 2: 41) or finely retouched bladelets.

Generally, it can be said that the middle Danubian Epigravettian is characterized by a fairly strong variability of lithic assemblages in the period from 19.000 to 17.000 years B.P. As far as technology is concerned their variability is the effect of using different raw materials. The boundary runs between assemblages using radiolarite river pebbles of small size (e.g. Sagvar and, partly, Grubgraben) and assemblages where bigger nodules of, for example, obsidian in the case of Kašov (upper level) were processed into blanks. As far as morphology of retouched tools is concerned assemblages differ as to the extent in which gravettian features disappeared (e.g. backed blades and points) and were replaced by "epi-Aurignacian" (e.g. high end-scrapers, ca-renoidal cores) and "epi-palaeolithic" (e.g. short and sub-circular end-scrapers) features.

REFERENCES

ABSOLON K. 1947. Paleoethnologická stavba velkých středoevropských diluviálnich stanic. Příroda, XL, 1-10

ANDRUSOV D. 1932.: O čtvrtohorních terasách Oravy a středního toku Váhu a několik, poznámek o geomorfologii západních Karpat slovenských. Věstník Státního Geologického Ústavu ČSR. 8:4, 244-257.

AMBROŽ V., LOŽEK V., PROŠEK F. 1952. Mladý pleistocén v okolí Moravan u Piešťan nad Váhom. Antropozoikum I, 53-142.

ALEXANDROWICZ S. W. 1987. Analiza malakalogiczna w badaniach osadów czwartorzędowych. *Kwart. AGH Geologia*, 12 (1-2); 1-240.

ALEXANDROWICZ S. W. 1988. Malacofauna of the Late Quaternary loess-like deposits in the Polish Carpathians. *Acta Geol. Pol.*, 38, 85-106.

ALEXANDROWICZ S. W. 1991. Malakofauna i wiek lessów z Maszkowa w dolinie Dłubni. *Wyd. Nauk. UAM Geografia*, 50, 379-387.

BÁNESZ L., HROMADA J., DESBROSSE R., MARGERAND I., KOZŁOWSKI J. K., SOBCZYK K., PAWLIKOWSKI M. 1992 Le site de plein air du Paléolithique supérieur de Kašov 1 en Slovaquie orientale. *Slovenská Archeológia* XL-1, 5-28.

BANNER J. 1960. Zu der Veröffentlichung des ersten paläolitischen Fundes in Mitteleuropa. Archeologické rozhledy, 12, 295-313.

BÁRTA J. 1960. K problematike listovitých hrotov typu Moravany-Dlhá. *Slovenská archeológia*, 8, 295-213.

BÁRTA J. 1965. *Slovensko v staršej a strednej dobe kamennej.* Bratislava.

BÁRTA J. 1970. Sídliská zo staršej doby kamennej na okolí Moravian nad Váhom. *Almanach Balnéologického Múzea v Piešťanoch*, V, 31-40.

BÁRTA J. 1972. Jaskyňa Čertova Pec pri Radošine. *Slovenský kras*, 10, 73-85.

BÁRTA J., 1984. Znovuobjavenie Moravianskej venuše. *Balneologický Spravodaj 1983*, 77-88.

BÁRTA J., 1986. Trenčiánske Bohuslavice vo svetle archeológie a histórie. *Krásy Slovenska*, LXIII/11, 16-21.

BÁRTA J., 1987 Problems of Dwellings Structures in the Palaeolithic of Western Slovakia. *Anthropologie* XXV/2, 105-110.

BARTA J., 1989 Trenčiánske Bohuslavice, un habitat gravettien en Slovaquie occidentale. *L'Anthropologie* 93:1, 173-182.

BAUR B., 1984. Shell size and growth rate differences for alpine population of *Arianta arbustorum* (L.). *Rev. Suis. Zool.* 91; 37-46.

BIAŁOBOK S., HELLWIG Z. 1955 *Drzewoznawstwo.* PWRiL. Warszawa

BINFORD L., 1980 Willow Smoke and Dog's Tail: Hunter-Gatherer Settlement Systems and Archaeological Site Formation. *American Antiquity* 45.

BUGAŁA W. 1975 Cis (*Taxus L.*) Systematyka i zmienność. In: *Cis pospolity Taxus baccata.* Ed. S. Białobok. *Nasze drzewa leśne* PWN. Warszawa– Poznań, t. II, 18-38.

DAVIS S. J. M. 1987 *The Archaeology of Animals.* B. T. Batsford Ltd, London.

DESBROSSE R., KOZŁOWSKI J. K. 1994 *Les habitats préhistoriques.* CTHS. Kraków–Paris.

DOBOSI V. T. 1992 A New Upper Palaeolithic Site at Mogyorósbánya. *Communicationes Archaeologicae Hungariae*, 5-16.

EISNER J. 1926. Studium předhistorické archeologie na Slovensku po převratě. Sborník Muzeálnej Spoločnosti Slovenska, XX, 14-25.

EISNER J. 1933. *Slovensko v pravěku.* Bratislava.

EISNER J. 1935. Prehistorický výskum na Slovensku a v Podkarpatské Rusi roku 1934. *Sbornik Muzeálnej Spoločnosti Slovenska*, XXIX, 51-80.

EISNER J. 1944-48. Predhistorický a protohistorický výskum na Slovensku a v Zakarpatskej Ukrajine v rokoch 1918-1938. *Sbornik Muzeálne spoločnosti Slovenska*, XXXVIII-XLII, 17-41.

EKS [Kubica-Sekera E.] 1943. Pri Piešťanoch vykopali najkrajšie náradie zo staršej doby kamennej. *Slovák*, 15.9.1943, Bratislava.

FALTYS F. 1946. Lovci mamutov v Piešťanoch. Práca, Bratislava,

FERENCZI S. 1917. Die geologischen Verhältnisse des Inovec-Gebirges südlich von Pöstyén. In: *Jahresbericht der königlich ungarischen Reichsantstalt für 1915;* Budapest, 142-174.

FOLTINY S. 1973. Ein slowakischer Bronzediademtyp in Metropolitan Museum of Art in New York. In *Zborník Filozofickej fakulty Univerzity Komenského-Musaica*, XX/XIII, 89-97.

GABORI M. 1959. Résultat de fouilles récemment effectuées dans la station paléolithique de Sagvar. *Arch. Ert.* 86.

GEYER D. 1927. *Unsere Land- und Süsswaser-Mollusken.* Lutz Verl. Stuttgart.

HAESAERTS P. 1990. Stratigraphy of the Grubgraben loess sequence. In: *The Epigravettian Site of Grubgraben, Lower Austria: the 1986 and 1987 Excavations.* Eraul 40. Liège.

HAJNALOVÁ E., KRIPPEL E. 1984. Katalóg paleobotanických nálezov z paleolitu Slovenská. In : *Acta Interdisciplinaria Archeologica*, III, Nitra, 304-314.

HAUER F. 1864. Antiquarische Funde aus Morovan. *Jahrbuch der Geologischen Reichanstalt*, 5, Wien.

HAUER 1871. Vorlage von prähistorischen Culturresten. *Mitteilungen der anthropologischen Gesellschaft in Wien*, I, Wien, 30-37.

HROMADA J. BÁNESZ L. KOZŁOWSKI J. SOBCZYK K. 1993: Výskum epigravettienskej stanice v Moravanoch nad Váhom-Žakovskej. *Archeologické výskumy a nálezy na Slovensku v roku 1992*, Nitra, 52-55.

HROMADA J. BÁRTA J. 1992. Výskum mladopaleolitickej stanice s radiolaritovou industriou v Moravanoch nad Váhom-Žakovskej. *Archeologické výskumy a nálezy na Slovensku v roku 1991*, Nitra, 51-53.

HROMADA, J. CUPER J. 1992. Nové nálezy štiepanej kamennej industrie z Moravian nad Váhom. *Archeologické výskumy a nálezy na Slovensku v roku 1990,* Nitra, 44-45.

HYNIE O. 1927. Geologická stavba širšího okolí lázni Piešťan a jejich termálni zřídla. *Sborník Státního Geologického Ústavu Československé Republiky,* VII, Praha, 619-650.

JAECKEL S. G. 1962. *Ergänzungen und Berichtigungen zum rezenten und quartären Vorkommen der mitteleuropäischen Mollusken.* Quelle & Meyer Verl. Leipzig.

KAMINSKA L. 1991. Význam surovinovej základne pre mladopaleolitickú spoločnosť vo východokarpatskej oblasti. *Slovenská Archeológia* XXXIX-1-2, 7-58

KASPAREK M. V. 1934. Altsteinzeitliche Funde aus der Slowakei. *Sudeta,* X, 1-2, München, 33-36.

KASPAREK M. V. 1935. Mammuthfunden im mittleren Waagtal. *Tagesbote* (Brno), 4.1. 1935,

KLEMM W. 1973. Die Verbreitung der rezenten Land-Gehäse-Schnecken in Österreich. *Denkschr. Öst. Akad. Wiss.,* 117: 3-503.

KNEBLOVA V. 1960. Paleobotanický výzkum interglacialnich travertinu v Gánovcich. *Biologické práce. Edicia Sekcie Biologických a Lekárskych Vied.* Slovenska Akadémia Vied, VI, 4, 5-42.

KOZŁOWSKI J. K. 1982. Technological and Typological Differentiation of Lithic Assemblages in the Upper Palaeolithic: An Interpretation Attempt. In: *Unconventional Archaeology, New Approach and Goals in Polish Archaeology,* Wrocław, 33-57.

KOZŁOWSKI J. K. 1986, The Gravettian in Central and Eastern Europe. *Advances in World Archaeology,* 5, 131-200.

KOZŁOWSKI J. K. 1986a. Changes in Raw Material Economy of the Gravettian Technocomplex in Northern Central Europe. In: *International Conference on Prehistoric Flint Mining.* Budapest, 65-80.

KRÓL S. 1975. Zarys ekologii. In: *Cis pospolity Taxus boccata.* red. S. Białobok. *Nasze drzewa leśne.* PWN, Warszawa-Poznań, t.II, 78-103.

KUBIAK H. 1987. Remains of Fossil Mammals. In: Kozłowski J. K., Sobczyk K. *The Upper Palaeolithic Site Kraków-Spadzista Street C2. Excavations 1980,* 93-96.

LEROI-GOURHAN A. 1976. L'habitat au Paléolithique supérieur. In: Colloque 13: *Les structures d'habitat au Paléolithique Superieur.* 9e Congrès U.I.S.P.P. Nice.

LEROI-GOURHAN A., BREZILLON M., 1972. *Fouilles de Pincevent. Essai d'analyse ethnographique d'un habitat magdalénien (la section 36).* 2v. 7e suppl. à Gallia Préhistoire.

LEROI-GOURHAN Arl. 1980. Les industries du Würm supérieur. In: *Problèmes de la stratigraphie quaternaire en France et dans les pays limitrophes.* Suppl. Bulletin AFEC N. S., vol. 1, 192-194.

LOŽEK V. 1949. Nové výzkumy v jižní části Považského Inovce. *Ochrana přírody,* IV, 6, 130-134.

LOŽEK V. 1960. K současné problematice stratigrafie mladopleistocénních spraší a časového zařazení mladého paleolitu. *Archeologické rozhledy,* 12, 560-575.

LOŽEK V. 1964. *Quartärmollusken der Tschechoslowakei.* Rozpr. U. U. G., 31, 3-374.

LOŽEK V. 1965. Das Problem der Lössbildung und die Lössmollusken. *Eizeitalt. u. Gegenwart,* 16, 61-75.

LOŽEK V. TYRÁČEK J. 1960. Příspěvek k poznání vývoje údolí Váhu mezi Trenčínem a Piešťany. *Sbornik Československé společnosti zeměpisné,* 65, 6-14.

LUSCHAN, F. 1876: Die Funde von Morovan. *Mitteilungen der anthropologischen Gesellschaft in Wien*, 6, 293-294.

MACHATSCHEK, F. DANZER M. 1924. Geologische und morpholo-gische Beobachtungen in den Westkarpathen. *Lotos*, 72, 39-80.

MÁDL J. 1936. Nález medených platní v Kočovciach, okr. Nové Mesto nad Váhom. *Sborník Muzeálnej Spoločnosti Slovenská*, 110-111.

MAMAKOWA K. STARKEL L., 1977. Stratigraphy of the Eo- and Mesoholocene Alluvia in Podgrodzie upon Wisłoka River. *Studia Geomorphologica Carpato-Balcanica*, 11.

MASON S. L. R., HATHER J. G., HILLMAN G. C. 1994. Preliminary Investigation of the Plant Macro-Remains from Dolní Věstonice II and Its Implications for Paleolithic Europe. *Antiquity* 68, No 258, 48-57.

MICKO A., 1943/1944. Die Ausgrabungen Moravany 1943. *Altböhmen und Altmähren*, 3/4, 35-42.

MONTET-WHITE A., 1990. The Archaeological Levels, Features and Spatial Distribution. In: *The Epigravettian Site of Grubgraben, Lower Austria: the 1986 and 1987 Excavations.* ERAUL 40, Liège, 47-64.

NOVOTNÁ M. 1973. Einige Bemerkungen zur Datierung der Kupferindustrie in der Slowakei. *Zborník Filozofickej fakulty Univerzity Komenského - Musaica XX/XIII, Bratislava, 5-21.*

PAWLIKOWSKI M., 1990. Mineralogical analysis of the loess samples In: *The Epigravettian site of Grubgraben, Lower Austria*: the 1986-1987 excavations. ERAUL 40. Liège, 37-47.

PAWLIKOWSKI M., 1992. *Petroarcheologia.* Skrypty AGH nr 1321. Kraków.

POKORNÝ J., 1967. *Bäume und Sträucher.* Artia. Praha.

PROŠEK F. 1950. Zjišťovací výzkum na paléolitické stanici v Moravanech na Slovensku. *Archeologické rozhledy, 2, 175-183.*

PROŠEK F. LOŽEK V. 1954. Sprašový profil v Bance u Piešťan. *Anthropozoikum*, III, Praha, 301-323.

PROŠEK F. LOŽEK V. 1955. Výzkum sprašového profilu v Zamarovcích u Trenčína. *Anthropozoikum*, IV, Praha, 181-200.

RALSKA-JASIEWICZOWA M., 1980, *Late Glacial and Holocene Vegetation of the Bieszczady Mts. (Polish Eastern Carpathians).* PWN, Warszawa-Kraków, 2-201.

SKLENAŘ K., 1975. Palaeolithic and Mesolithic Dwellings: Problems of Interpretation. *Pamatky Archeologické* 2.

SKLENAŘ K., 1976 Palaeolithic and Mesolithic Dwellings: an Essay in Classification. *Pamatky Archeologické* 2.

SKUTIL J., 1934a. Moravany, eine Station des diluvialen Menschen bei Piešťany in der Slowakei. *Mitteilungen der Museumsgesellschaft, Piešťany*, Ausgabe Nr. 7, 1-4.

SKUTIL J., 1934b. Stanice diluviálního člověka v Moravanech u Piešťan na Slovensku. *Sdělení Museální Společnosti v Piešťanech*, Piešťany, Nr. 6, 1-4.

SKUTIL J., 1938. *Paleolitikum Slovenska a Podkarpatskej Rusi.* Turčiansky Sväty Martin.

SKUTIL J., 1957. Znovu k prvním paleolitickým nálezům v Karpatské oblasti *Študijné Zvesti Archeologického Ústavu Slovenskej Akadémie Vied v Nitre*, 2, 15-19.

SKUTIL J., 1959. Die Feststellung des mitteleuropäischen Paläolithikums die Tat der magyarischen Wissenschaft (Zum neuzigjährigen Jubileum). *Acta Archaeologica Academiae Scientarum Hungaricae*, IX, 49-52.

STARKEL L., 1983. Paleogeografia i klimat późnego plejstocenu i holocenu. In: *Człowiek i Środowisko w pradziejach*. Etd. J. K. Kozłowski, S. K. Kozłowski. PWN, Warszawa, 14-31.

SVOBODA J., 1994. *Paléolit Moravy a Slezska*. Brno.

ŚRODOŃ A., 1975. Historia cisa na naszych ziemiach. In: *Cis pospolity Taxus boccata*. Ed. S. Białobok. Nasze drzewa leśne. PWN, Warszawa-Poznań, t. II, 7-17.

TOMANEK J., 1987 *Botanika leśna*. PWRiL, Warszawa.

VELICHKO A. A., GREKHOVA L. V., GUBONINA Z. P., 1977. *Sreda obitania pervobytnogo cheloveka Timonovskich stoyanok*. Moskva: Nauka.

VITÁSEK F. 1932. Terasy horního Váhu. *Spisy odboru Československé Společnosti Zeměpisné v Brne* řada A, Brno, 4:23.

ZOTZ L. F. 1939. Neue Funde aus dem Aurignacien-Lössrastplatz von Moravany in der Slowakei. *Forschungen und Fortschritte*, 17, 204-205.

ZOTZ L. F. 1941a. Ein neuer Grossrastplatz der Mammutjäger bei Moravany in der Slowakei. *Wiener Prähistorische Zeitschrift*, 26, 52-57.

ZOTZ L. F. 1941b. Zwei Jahre Aufbauarbeit im Institut für Ur- und Frühgeschichte der Deutschen Karls-Universität in Prag. *Nachrichtenblatt für Deutsche Vorzeit*, 17, No 7-11, 165-174.

ZOTZ L. F. 1942. Der erste altsteinzeitliche Hausgrundriss in Mitelleuropa. *Quartär*, 4, 193-197.

ZOTZ L. F. 1951. *Altsteinzeitkunde Mitteleuropas*. Stuttgart.

ZOTZ L. F. 1968. Die Venusstatuette von Moravany nad Váhom. *Slovenská archeológia*, 16, 5-15.

ZOTZ L. F. VLK W. 1939. Das Paläolithikums des unteren Waagtales. *Quartär*, 2, 65-101.

PLATES

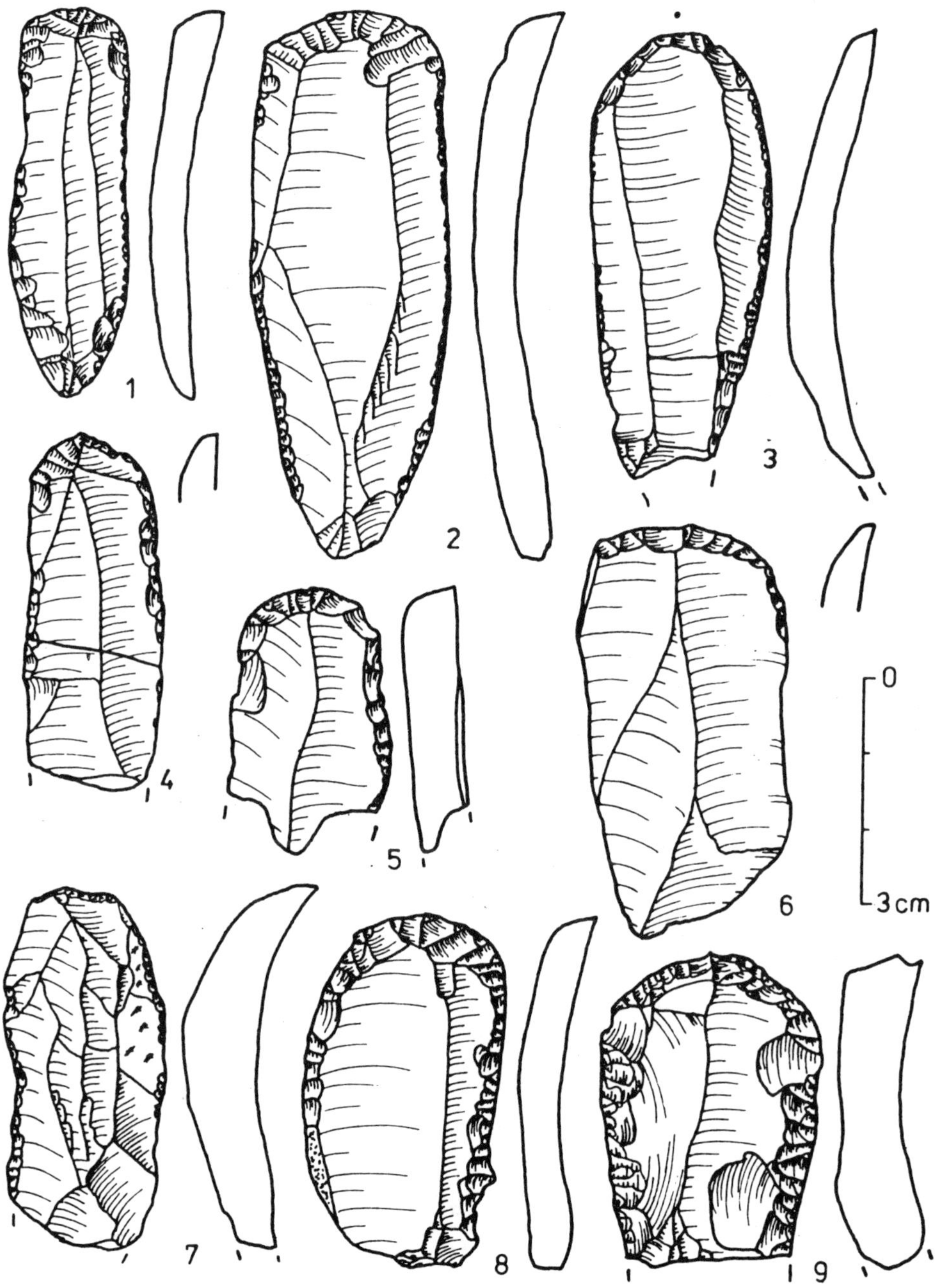

Pl. 1. Moravany-Žakovska. 1-9 – end-scrapers.

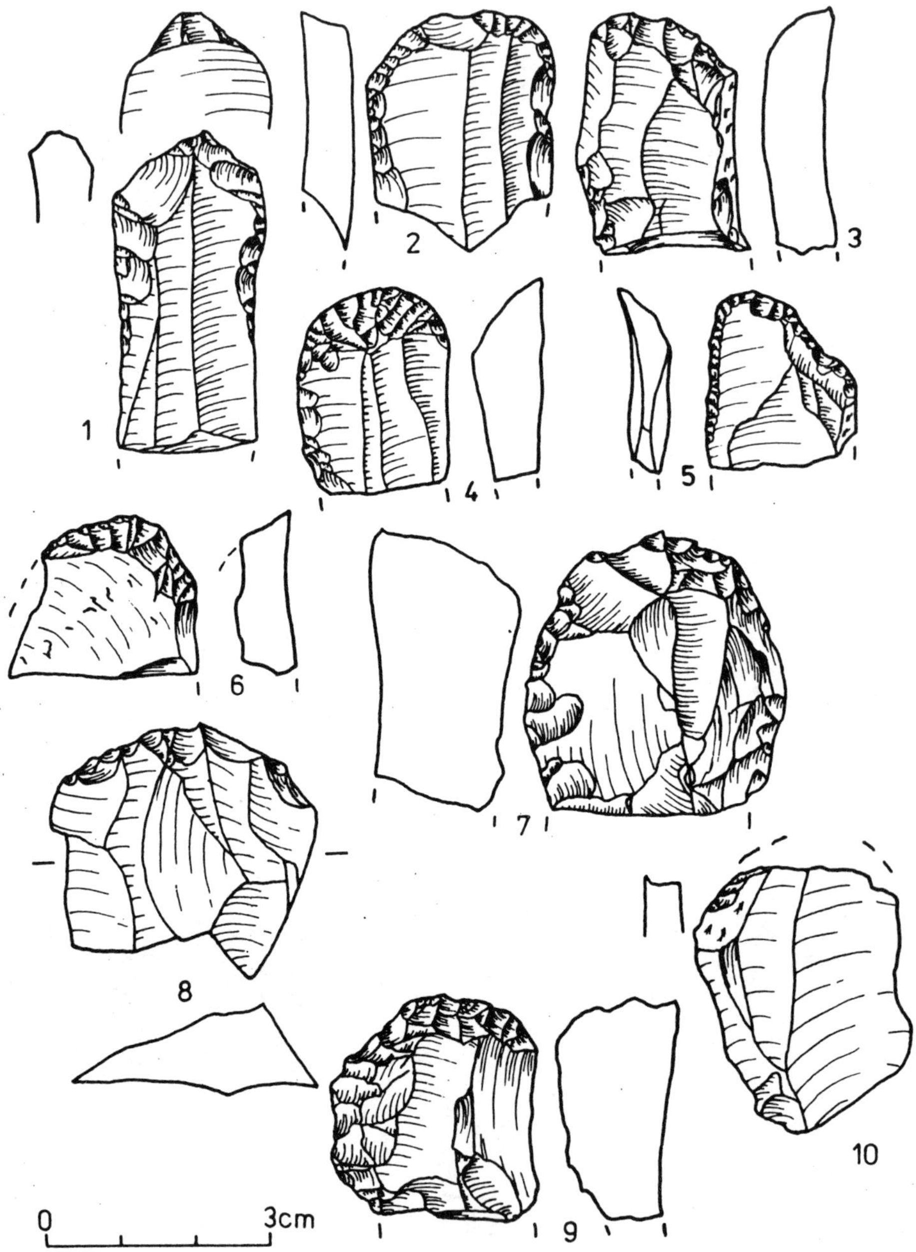

Pl. 2. Moravany-Žakovska. 1-10 – end-scrapers.

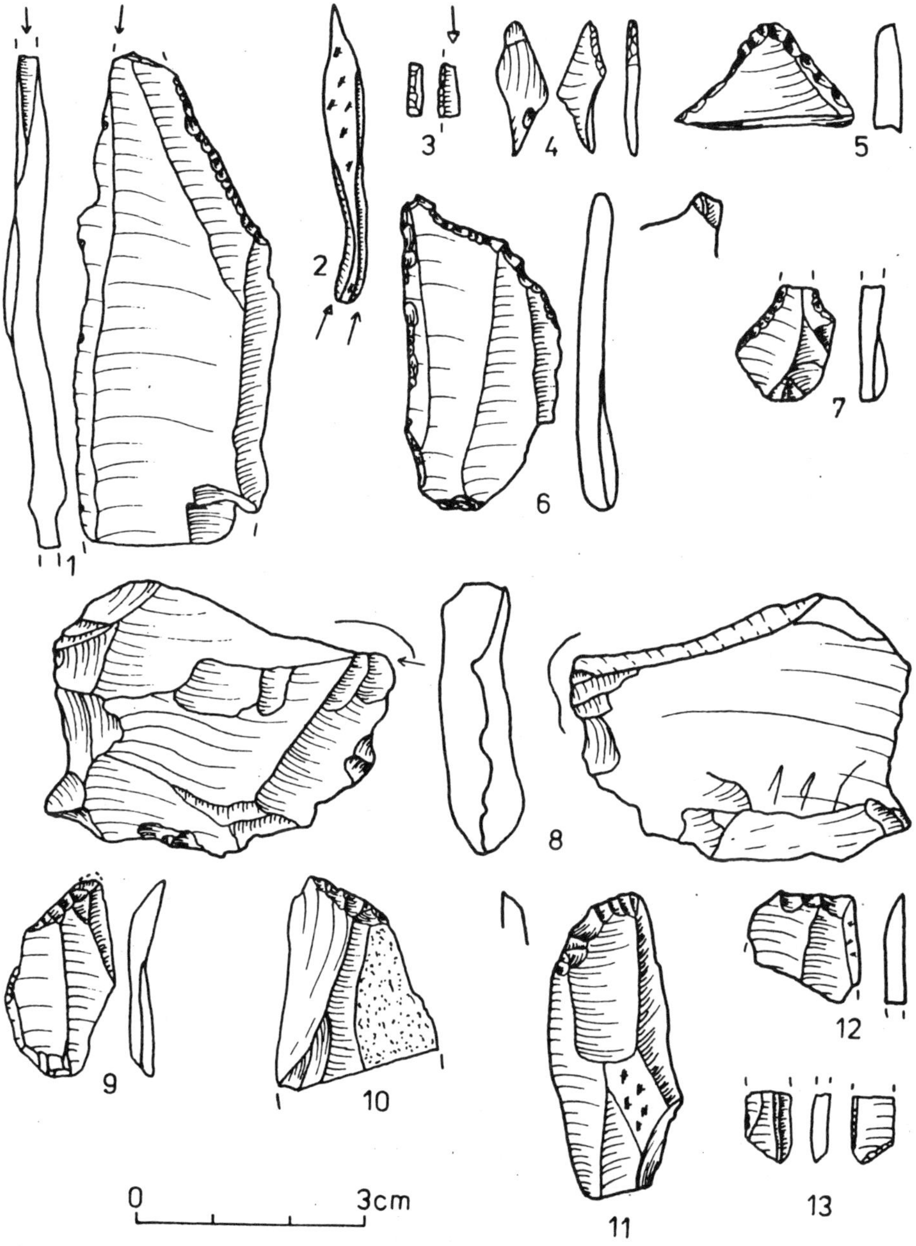

Pl. 3. Moravany-Žakovska. Burins (1,8), burin spalls (2-4), perforators (5-7), retouched truncations (9-13).

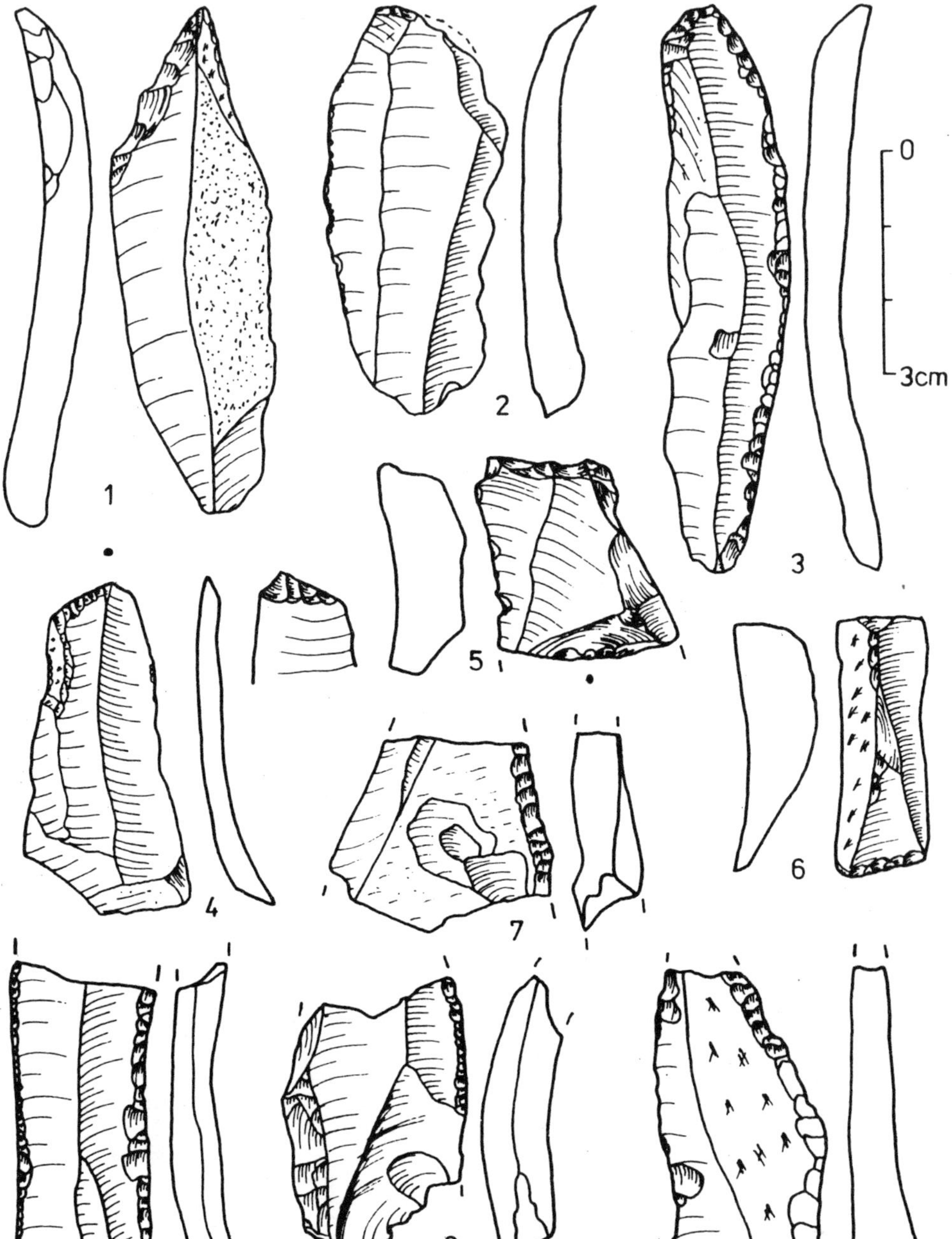

Pl. 4. Moravany-Žakovska. Retouched truncations (1,2,4,5,6) and retouched blades (3,7,8-10).

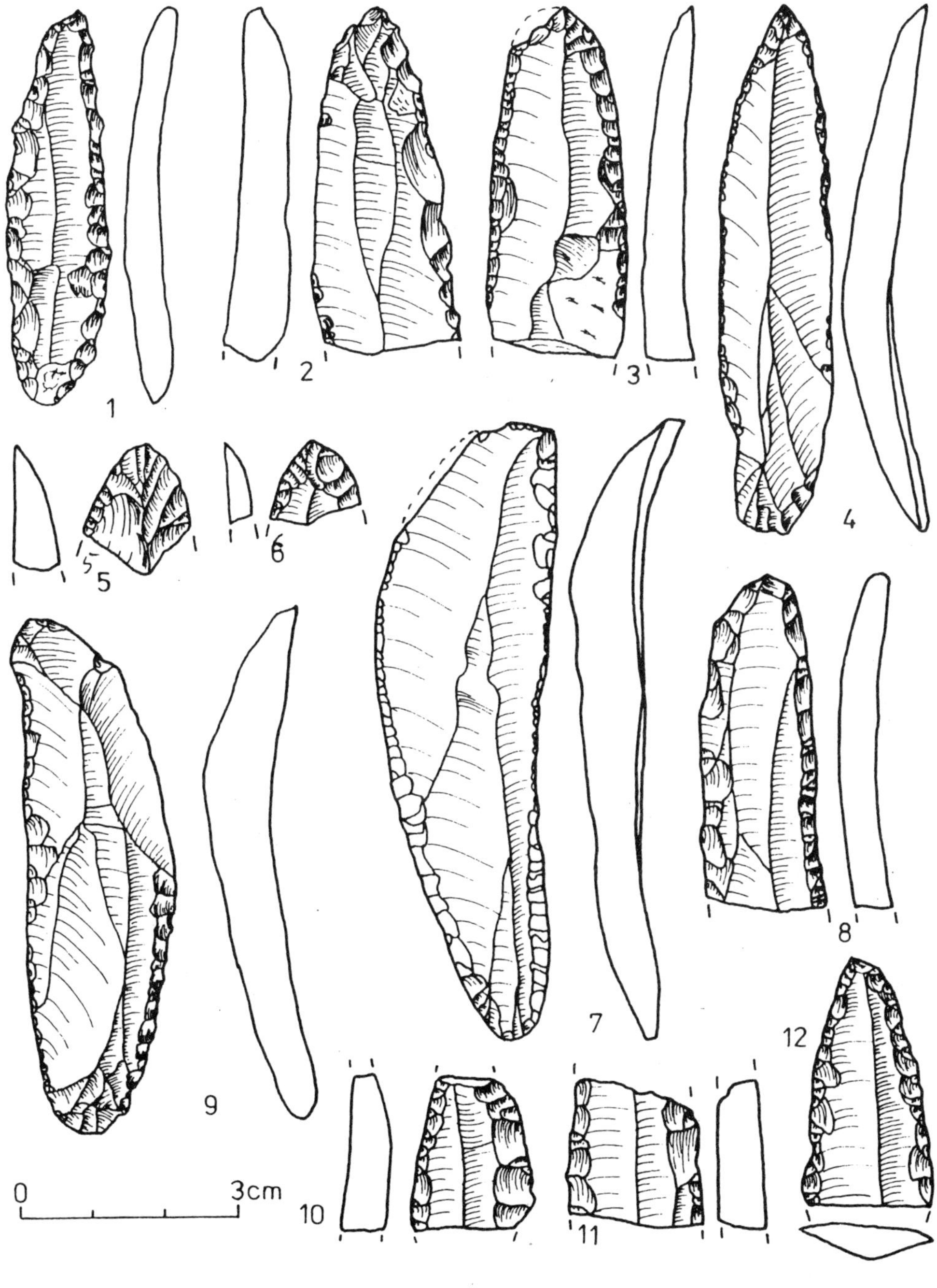

Pl. 5. Moravany-Žakovska. 1-12 – retouched blades.

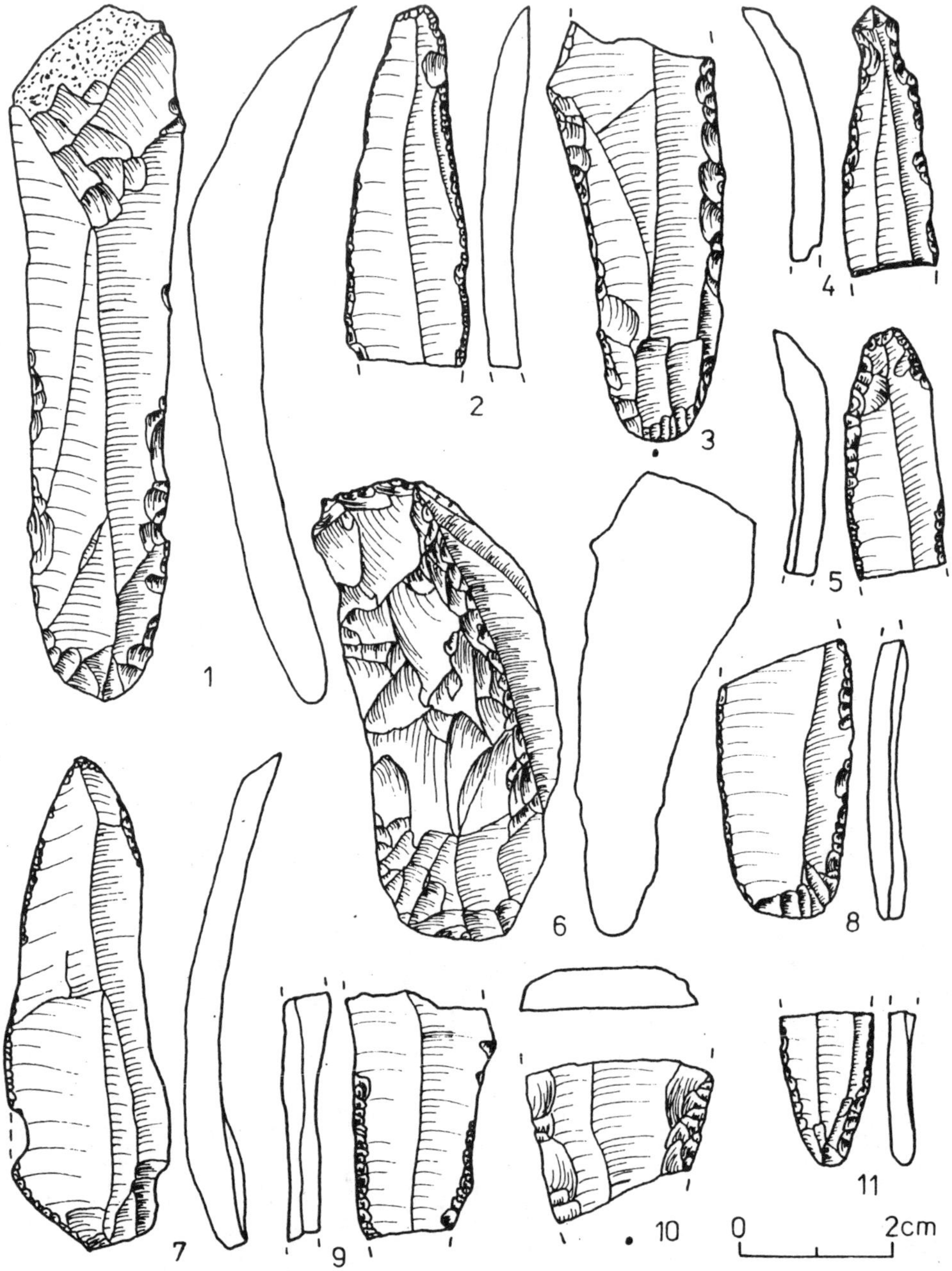

Pl. 6. Moravany-Žakovska. 1-11 – retouched blades.

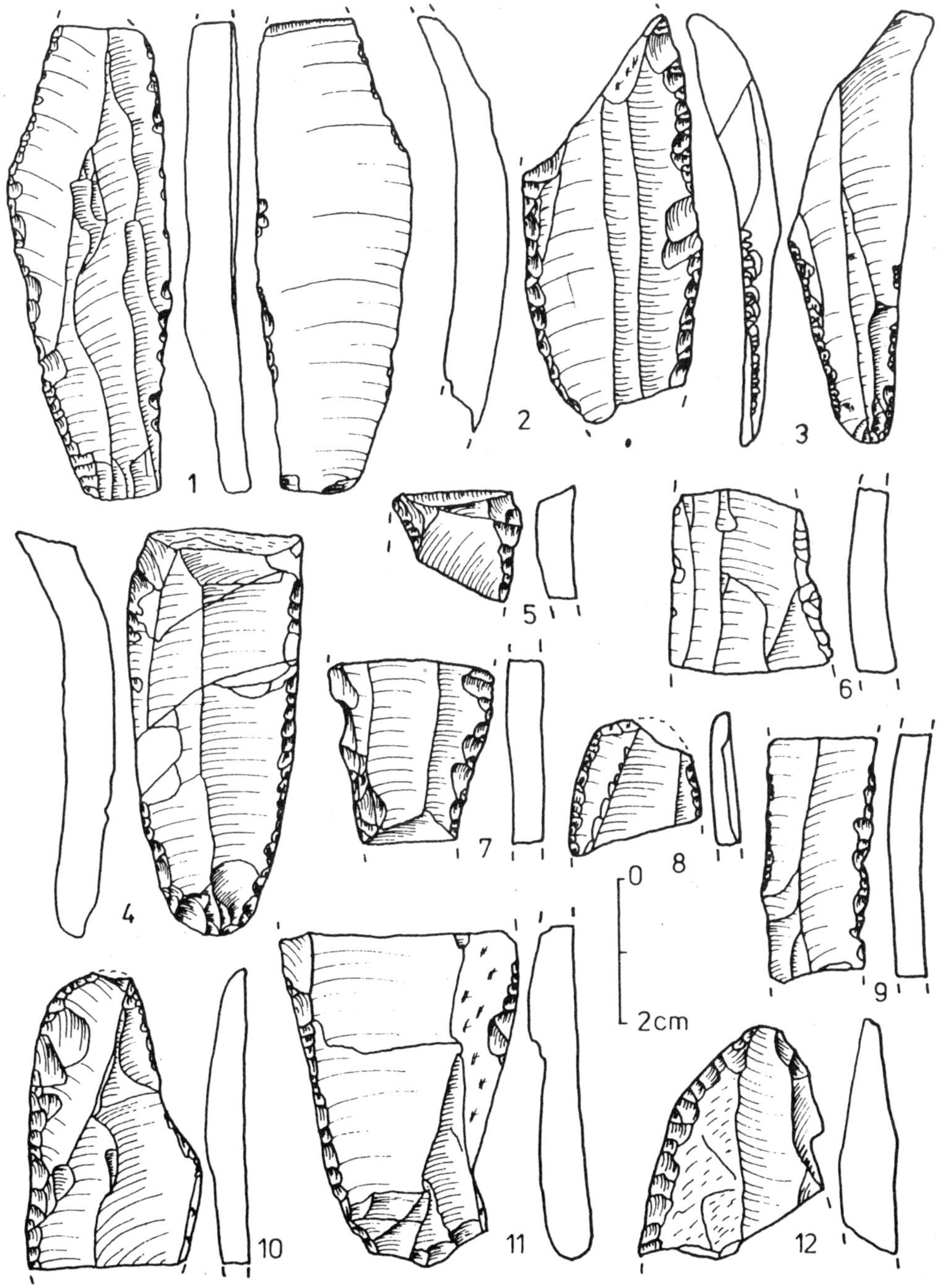

Pl. 7. Moravany-Žakovska. 1-12 – retouched blades.

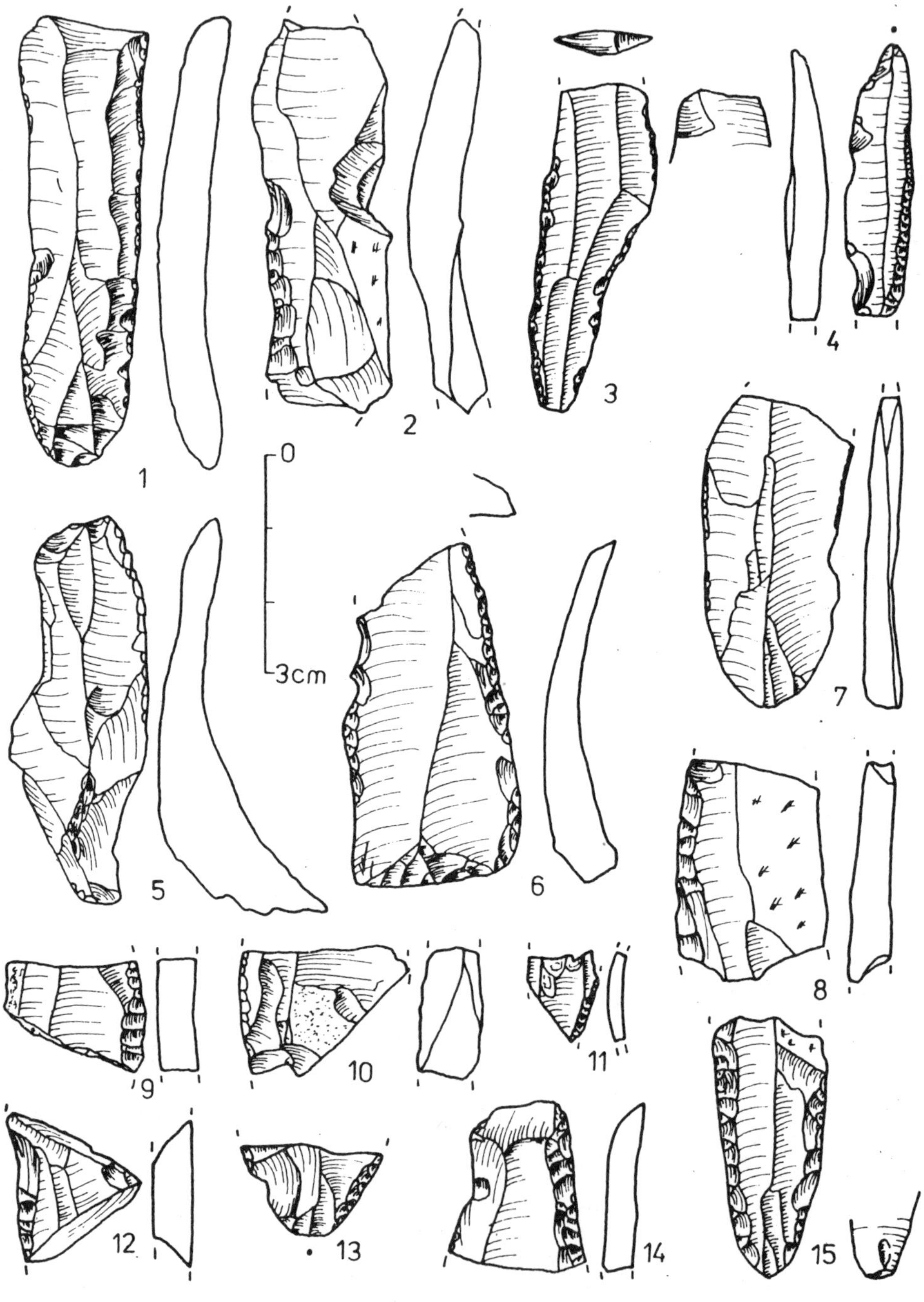

Pl. 8. Moravany-Žakovska. 1-15 – retouched blades.

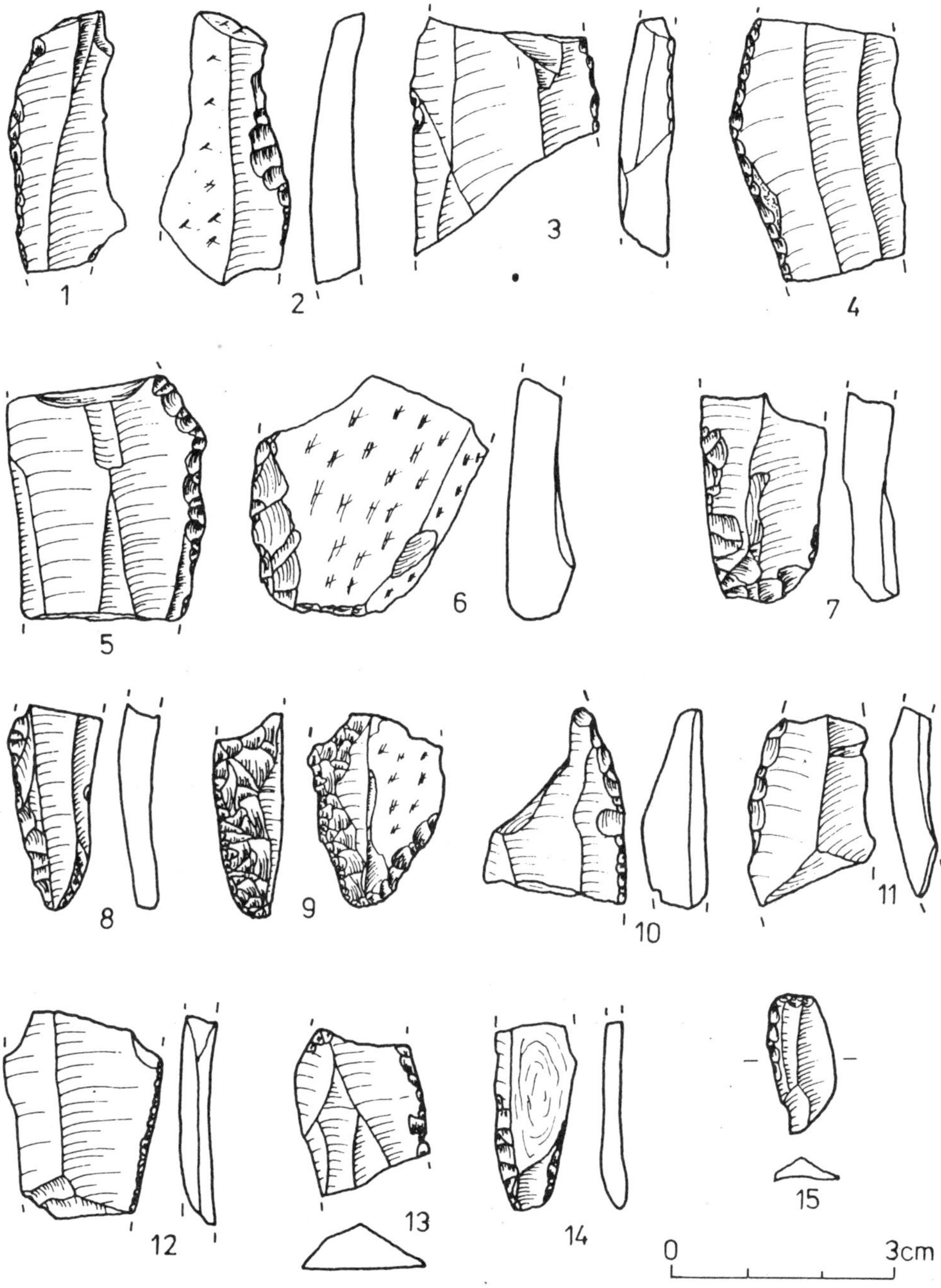

Pl. 9. Moravany-Žakovska. 1-15 – retouched blades.

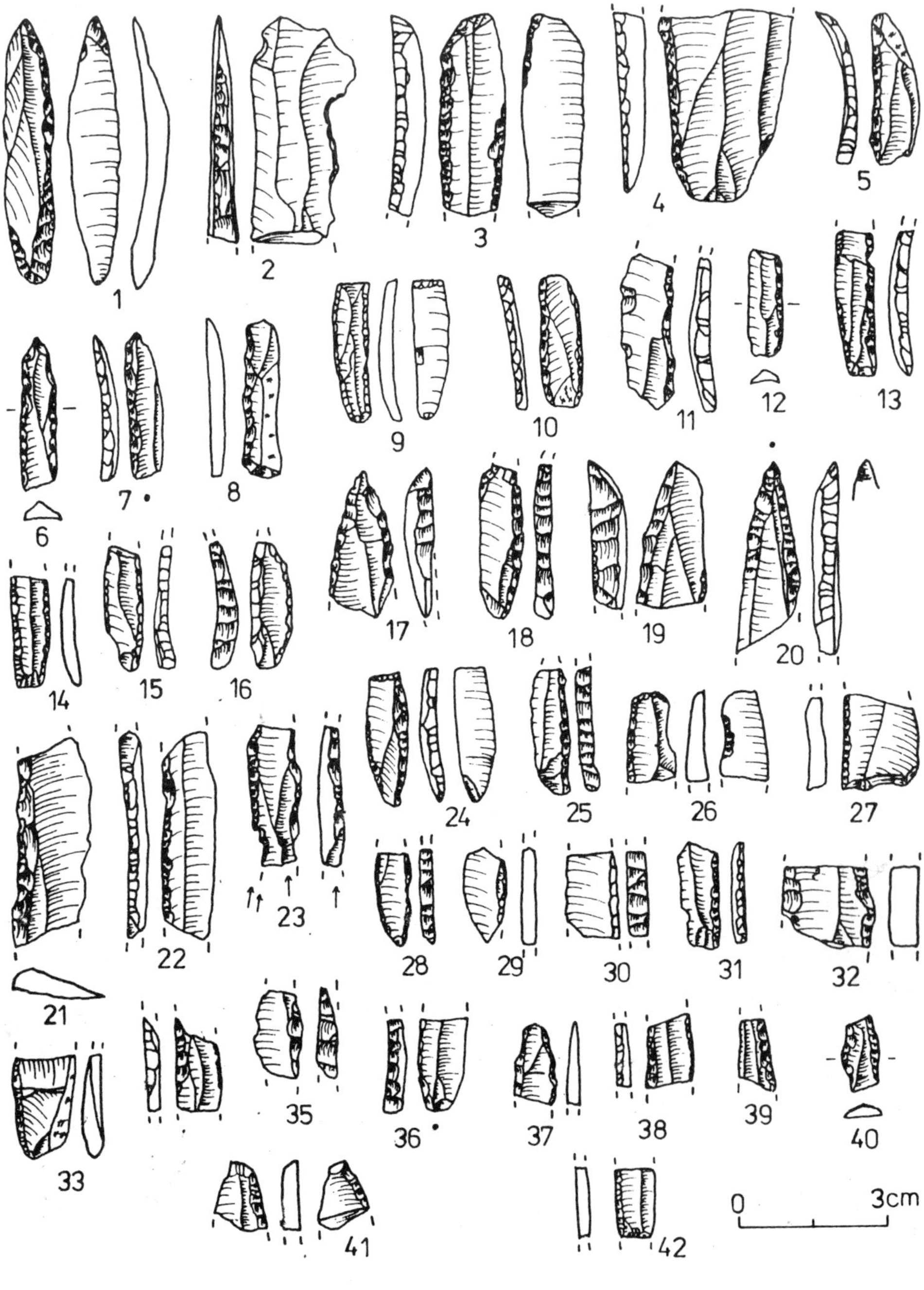

Pl. 10. Moravany-Žakovska. 1-42 – backed blades and bladelets (1 – microgravette point).

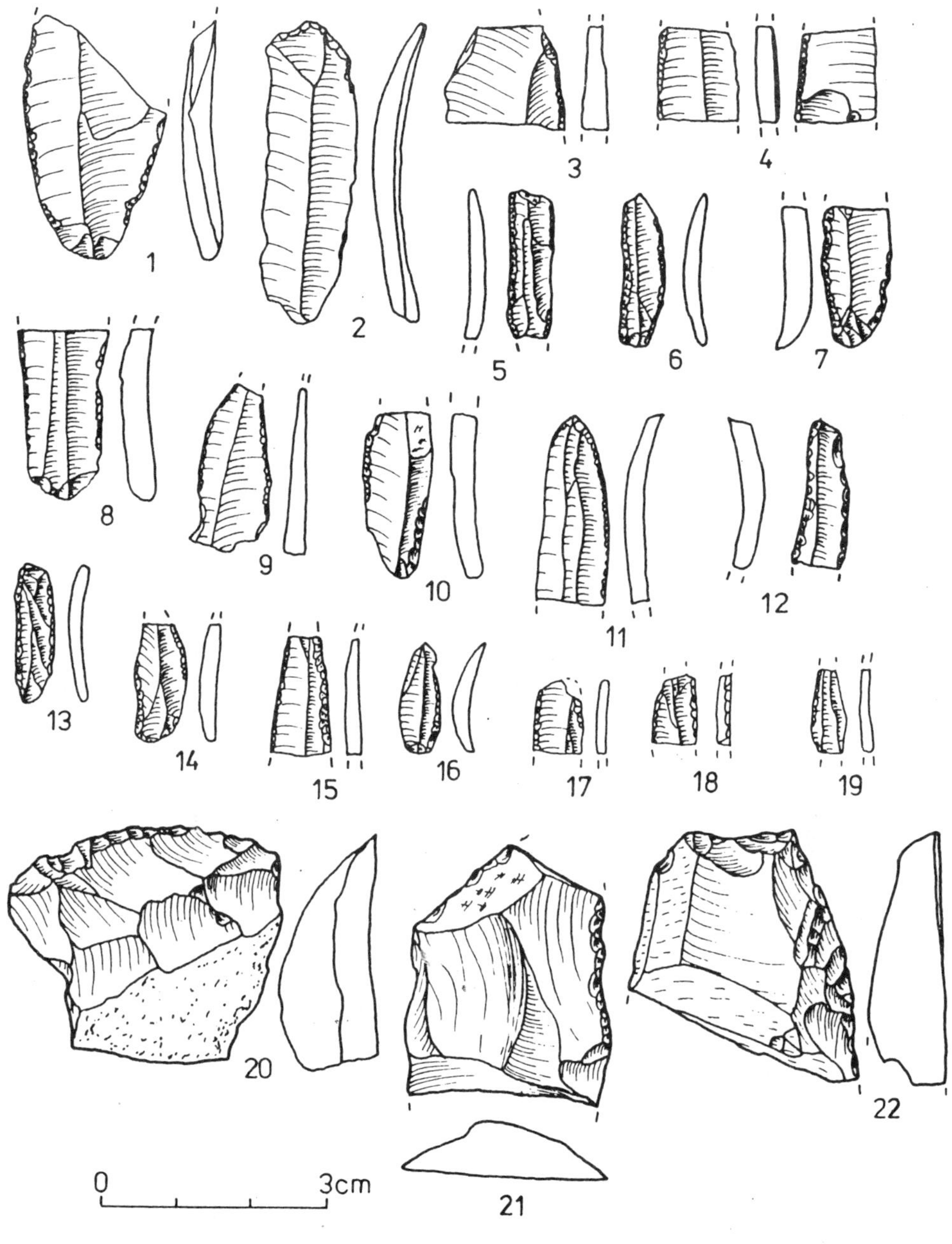

Pl. 11. Moravany-Žakovska. 1-19 – microretouched bladelets, 20-22 – side-scrapers.

Pl. 12. Moravany-Žakovska. 1-10 – retouched flakes, notched and denticulated tools.

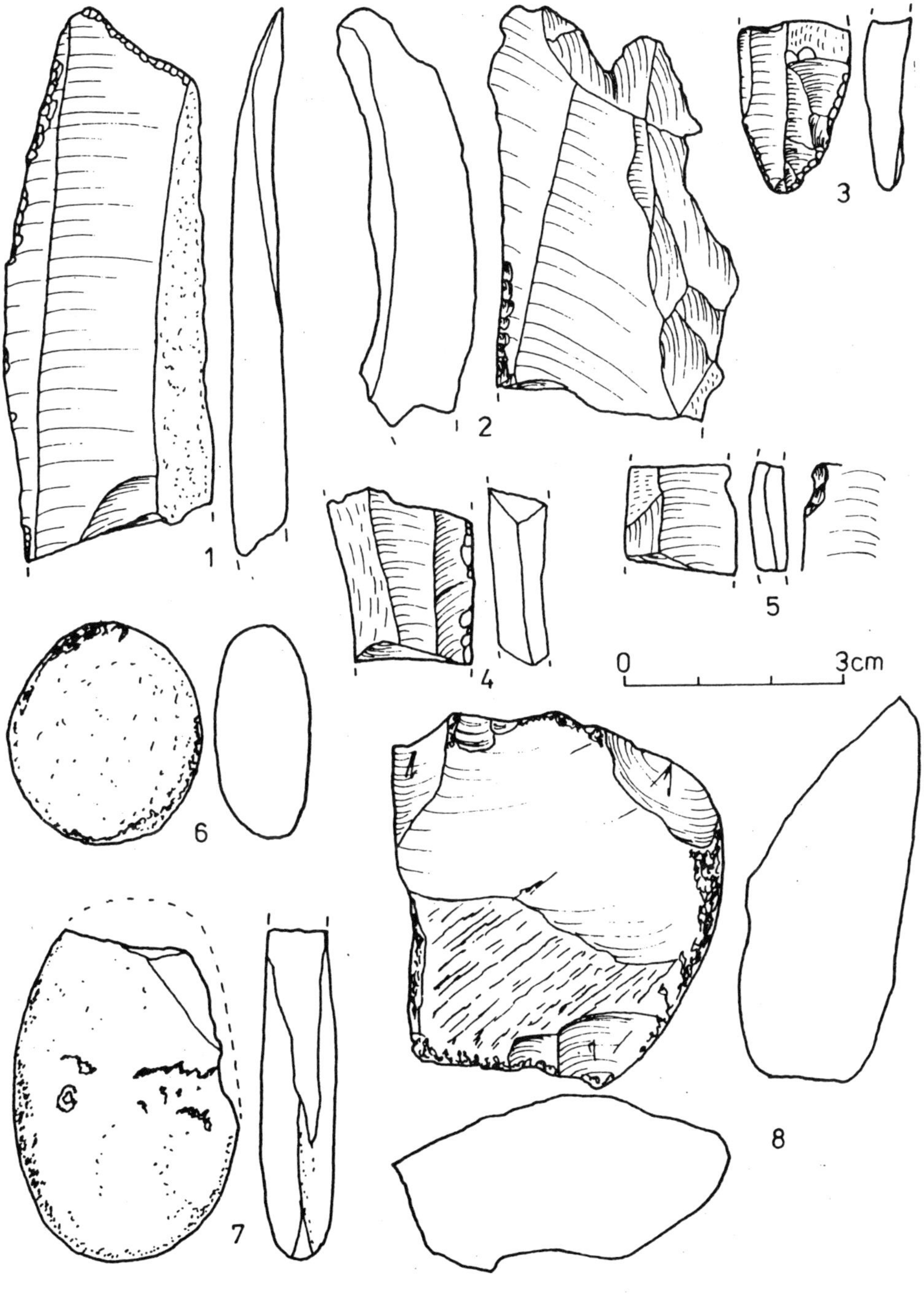

Pl. 13. Moravany-Žakovska. 1-8 – blades with macroscopic traces of use, 6 – pebble with traces of use, 7 – retoucher, 8 – hammerstone.

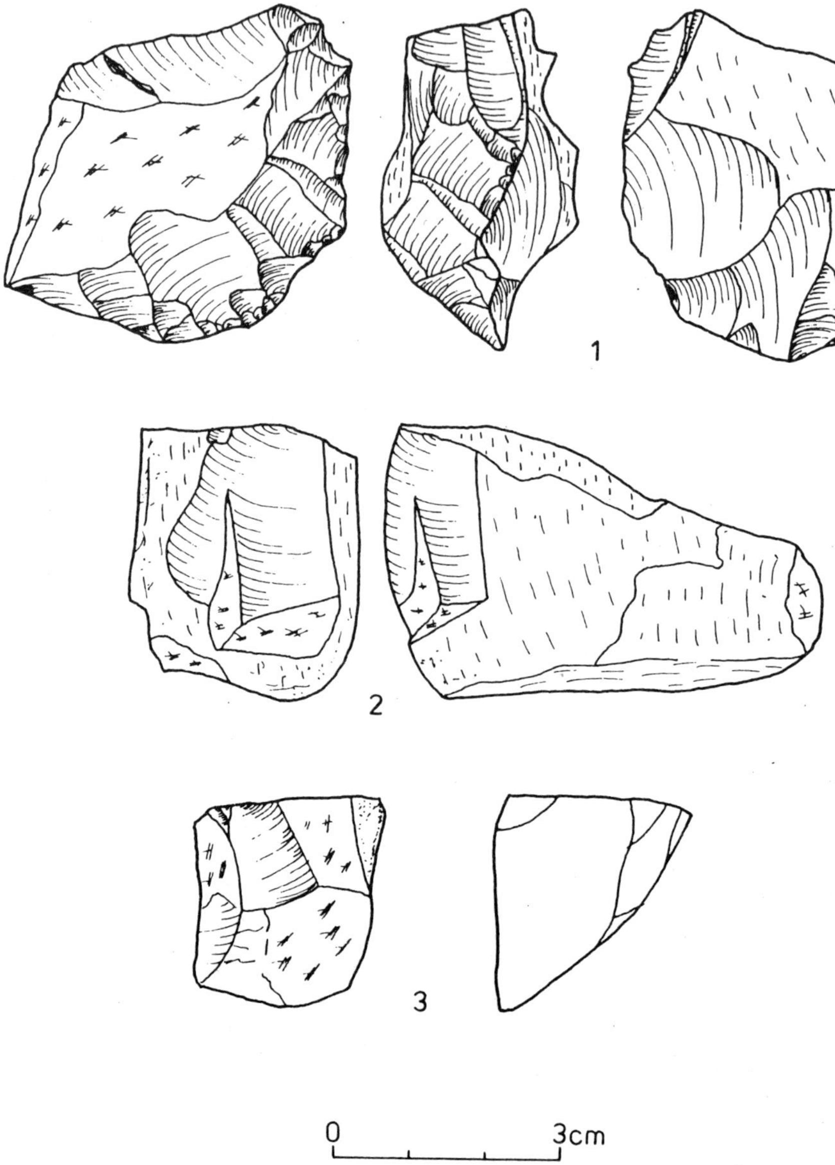

Pl. 14. Moravany-Žakovska, 1-3 – cores.

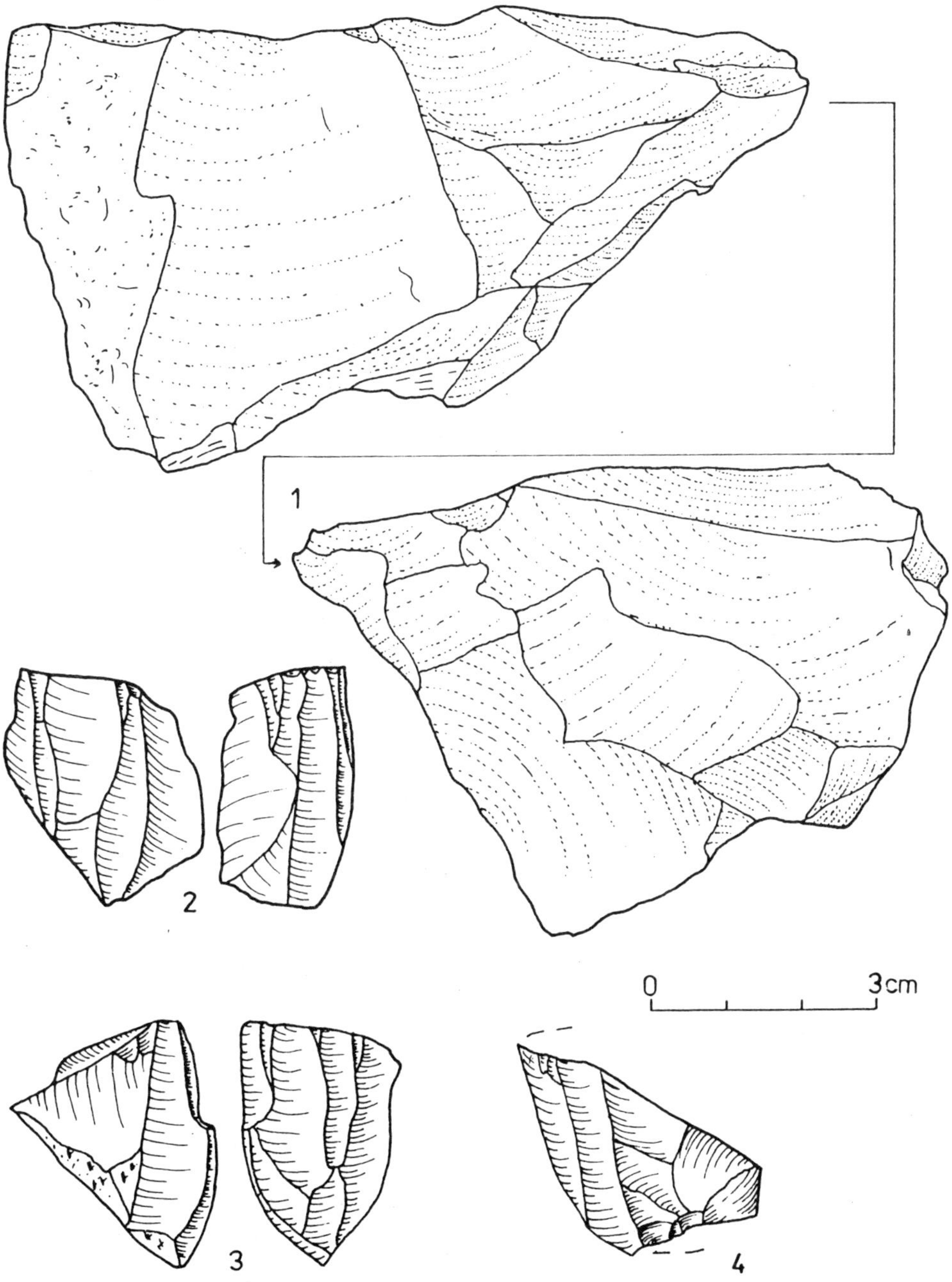

Pl. 15. Moravany-Žakovska. 1-4 – cores.

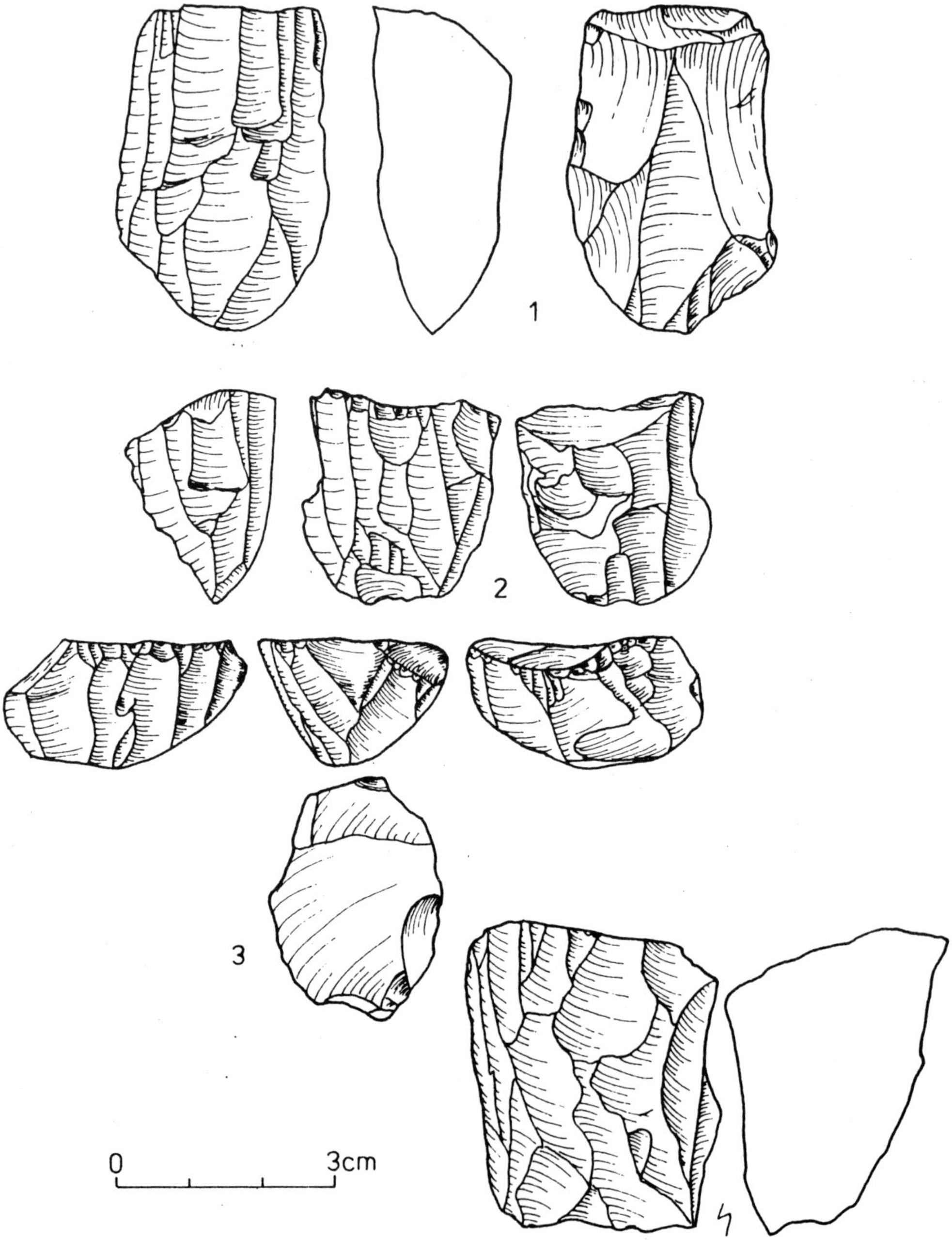

Pl. 16. Moravany-Žakovska. 1-4 – cores.

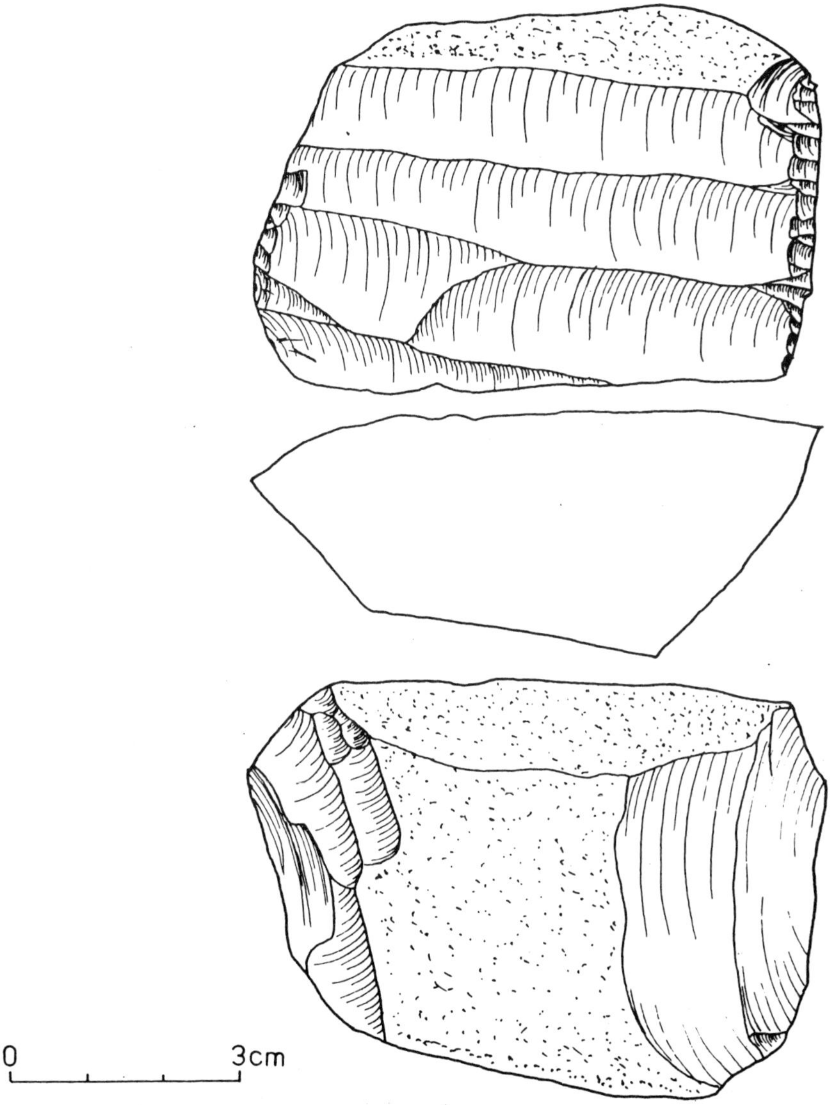

Pl. 17. Moravany-Žakovska. Core.

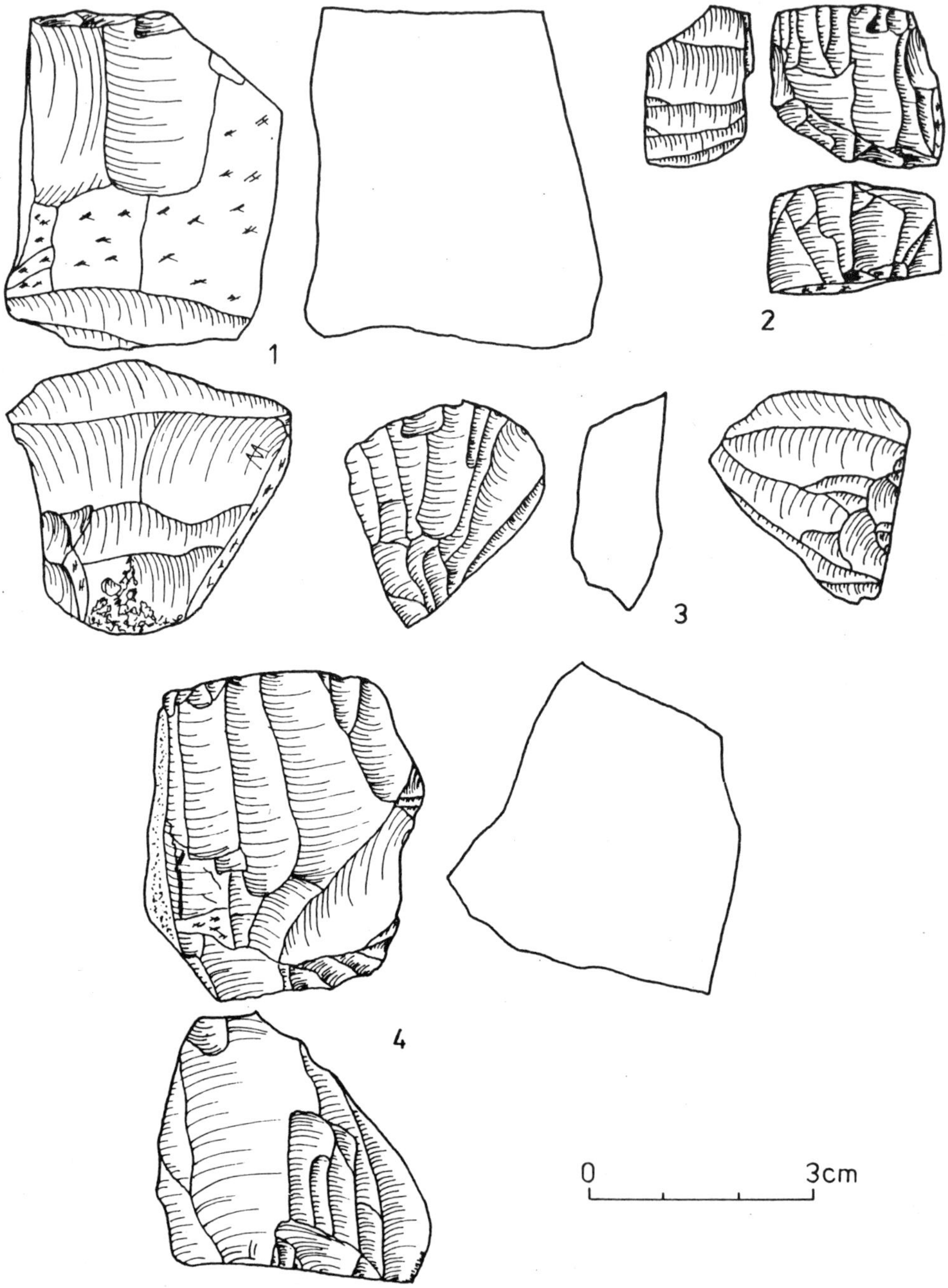

Pl. 18. Moravany-Žakovska. 1-4 – cores.

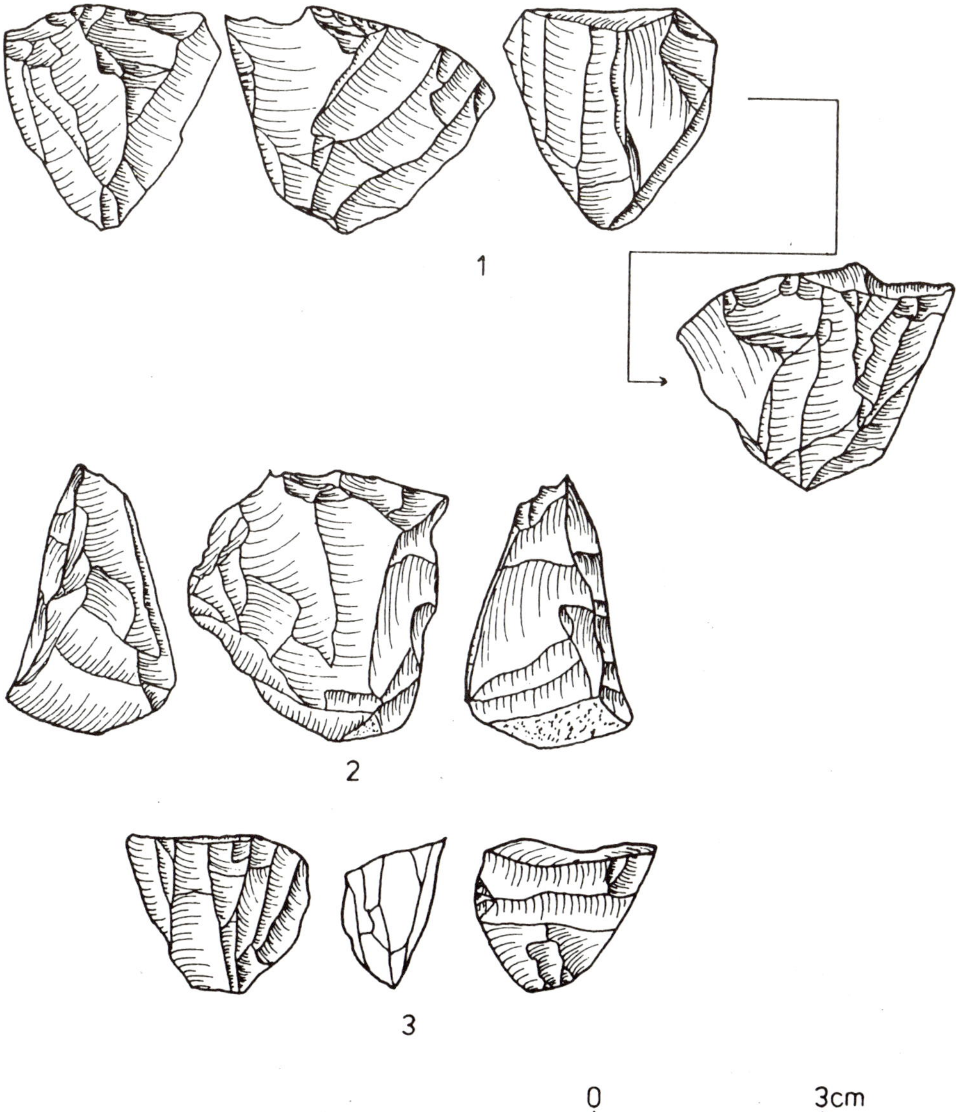

Pl. 19. Moravany-Žakovska. 1-3 – cores.